Leader Killers

How to Identify and Deal with Antagonists in Your Organization

Adv. Chr. Res.

Kenneth C. Haugk, Ph.D.

Tebunah Press • St. Louis, Missouri

Pastor
BV4502
2006
H38

Leader Killers: How to Identify and Deal with Antagonists in Your Organization

Tebunah Press
7053 Lindell Blvd.
St. Louis, MO 63130-4402

Copyright © 2006 by Kenneth C. Haugk

All rights reserved. Except for brief quotations in critical articles or reviews, no part of this book may be reproduced in any manner whatsoever without prior written permission from the publisher.

Adapted from *Antagonists in the Church: How to Identify and Deal with Destructive Conflict* © 1988 by Kenneth C. Haugk (Minneapolis: Augsburg Publishing House) by permission of Augsburg Fortress.

Printed in the United States of America

1 2 3 4 5 6 7 8 9 10

Library of Congress Cataloging-in-Publication Data is available.

ISBN: 0-9634093-1-X

*For all those who
love their jobs
and want to do them
effectively, efficiently, and in peace*

Contents

Acknowledgments 7
Is There an Antagonist in Your Midst?
Seven Questions 9

Part One: Identifying Antagonists

1. Who Are Antagonists? 15
2. Personality Characteristics of
   Antagonists 21
3. Red Flags of Antagonism 31
4. Recognizing the Tactics and
   Maneuvers of Antagonists 43
5. Levels of Organizational Conflict 57
6. Why Antagonism Happens 63
7. A Question of Values 69

Part Two: Dealing with Antagonists

8. Coping with Invisible Antagonists 77
9. Handling Indispensable Antagonists 81
10. Dealing with Antagonists in
    Group Settings 91
11. Mobilizing the Management Team 97
12. Four Specific Leadership Strategies 101

13. How to Handle a One-to-One Meeting
    with an Antagonist 109
14. Organizational Communications
    Regarding Antagonism 125
15. Personal and Family Variables 131
16. The Aftermath 137

Part Three: Preventing Antagonism

17. How to Create and Maintain an
    Anti-Antagonist Culture 145
18. Relating to Dormant Antagonists 151
19. Educating Others 159
20. The Last Temptation 163

Index 167

About the Author 173

Acknowledgments

Writing a book is rarely a solitary activity. Although my name appears on the cover of this book, many people contributed to the final product.

First, my sincere thanks to all those who shared with me their personal experiences with antagonists. In interviews and focus groups, in correspondence and consultations, and in conversations at seminars and workshops on dealing with antagonists, their stories emerged. For obvious reasons of confidentiality I can't name them, but my gratitude to each and every one of them is immense.

More than a hundred individuals, including several workplace study groups, gave excellent feedback on the manuscript in three separate rounds of reviews, and each time it came back better.

Those who have shared experiences in conversations and in reviewing the manuscript represent every level of management in large companies and small businesses, in both for-profit and not-for-profit sectors, government and private enterprise, health

Acknowledgments

care, sports, education, and a variety of other areas. The life and work experiences of the many who have faced antagonists give this book validity and immediacy that no amount of academic discussion ever could.

Special thanks to Stan Schroeder, who helped me steer a safe course around any legal shoals by his knowledgeable and direct comments.

The editing help of Scott Perry and Jeanette Rudder contributed greatly to the precision and clarity of this work. In addition, Lori Kem maintained the extensive database of research and reviewers as the manuscript went through numerous drafts and revisions.

Here's to your health and the health of the organization for which you work. May the illumination cast by all who have shared in the making of this book light your way.

Is There an Antagonist in Your Midst?

Seven Questions

*L*EADER KILLERS IS A TITLE THAT TAKES A STRONG STOMACH TO ACCEPT. Who are leader killers? They are antagonists—individuals whose behavior is characterized by tenacious divisiveness. If you have someone in mind who you think might qualify as the subject matter of this book, ask yourself these questions.

1. Is the person's behavior divisive? ❑ Yes ❑ No
2. Is the attack irrational? ❑ Yes ❑ No
3. Does he or she go out of the way to initiate trouble? ❑ Yes ❑ No
4. Are the person's demands insatiable? ❑ Yes ❑ No
5. Are the concerns upon which he or she bases the attack minimal or fabricated? ❑ Yes ❑ No

6. Does the person avoid causes that involve personal risk, suffering, or sacrifice?   ❏ Yes   ❏ No

7. Does the person's motivation appear selfish?   ❏ Yes   ❏ No

If your answers to several of these questions are yes, you have enough evidence to suggest that you have an antagonist on your hands, and you need to take a closer look. This book is devoted to that closer look and what to do about it.

This work is an outgrowth of an earlier book I wrote titled *Antagonists in the Church: How to Identify and Deal with Destructive Conflict.* As a pastor, I was seeing the injuries antagonists inflict on the church and had also personally experienced the full brunt of an antagonist's attack. As a clinical psychologist, I was working with pastors and family members who talked about the damage that antagonists had done to them, both personally and professionally. I started researching the topic, doing surveys and interviews with both pastors and lay leaders, and compiling the information. I began conducting workshops for church groups about antagonists and how to deal with them. Businesspeople who attended these workshops in connection with their churchly responsibilities or who had read *Antagonists in the Church* told me time and again, "This is not just a concern of the church. Antagonists exist everywhere." They began to invite me to speak at various business conferences and training events.

When I conduct seminars for business groups, I certainly do not hide my church connection, but neither do I belabor the issue. I think the connection is pertinent in one respect, however: If it is acceptable to deal with antagonists in religious settings—often thought of as "softer" environments—it is certainly all right to deal with them in business settings.

Jack Welch, former CEO of General Electric, calls these people "disrupters" in his book, *Winning*. They are "individuals who cause trouble for sport—inciting opposition to management for a variety of reasons, most of them petty." He adds, "They're poison."[1]

In addition to the workplace, antagonists turn up at school board meetings and in health care settings. You find them among parents at Little League games or band booster associations. They disrupt neighborhood associations and city council meetings, fraternities and sororities, churches and synagogues, as well as other volunteer organizations—in short, they can be anywhere.

Antagonistic behavior is also cross-cultural. Individuals from many other countries and cultures have attended workshops I've conducted on antagonism, and their descriptions of antagonists are very similar to the descriptions people of North America give.

Antagonists are not just misguided and misunderstood. They are out to hurt people, and they do. Sooner or later most organizations and most individuals—leaders or not—encounter antagonists. Antagonists, although few in number, have the potential for disproportionately disrupting or destroying the

---

[1] Jack Welch with Suzy Welch, *Winning* (New York: HarperBusiness, 2005), pp. 112–13.

efficiency and effectiveness of an organization as well as the peace of mind and well-being of the individuals within that organization.

If your organization has antagonists snapping at it, whether from within or without, its mission will be greatly compromised until the matter is recognized and action taken. You, your organization's leaders, and your staff can successfully deal with antagonists. The goal of this book is to equip you to detect and identify antagonists early, to deal with them effectively, and to prevent them from ever gaining a foothold. With such knowledge and skills in hand, you will be prepared if and when antagonists emerge.

By addressing antagonism, you and others joining with you will enhance staff productivity, decrease turnover, and save money for your organization. Dealing with antagonists truly is a bottom-line issue for any organization, and it's the right thing to do.

Part One

Identifying Antagonists

CHAPTER 1

Who Are Antagonists?

ANTAGONISTS ARE REAL. They leave in their wake roiled organizations, broken lives, and people who are hurt, discouraged, and disheartened. Business and organization leaders as well as all employees have enough to handle in their jobs without adding the burdens of antagonistic battles and disruption. Add to that evenings and weekends preoccupied with mental rehashings and endless-loop searches for solutions, and you have a recipe for burnout.

Antagonism in action is not pleasant. It is a harsh reality that must be reckoned with. Antagonists are abusive. They wantonly, selfishly, and destructively attack others. These attacks can result in repeated disruption of projects, deadlines, and priorities; they can mean loss of valuable staff, shortened careers, and lowered productivity.

Antagonism should not be confused with mere criticism or healthy conflict. People sometimes use the word *antagonists* to describe those on different sides in an argument. That is not the intended use in this book. For healthy conflict, organizations might do well to adopt the terminology of the British

Parliament, calling those in differing camps the "Honorable Opposition." Antagonism is unhealthy conflict, however, and antagonists are not honorable.

Defining the Issue

The word *antagonists* is defined and used throughout this book in this way:

> Antagonists are individuals who, on the basis of *nonsubstantive evidence, go out of their way* to make *insatiable demands,* usually *attacking* the person or performance of others. These attacks are *selfish in nature, tearing down rather than building up,* and are frequently directed against those in a leadership capacity.

Some key terms in this definition deserve closer attention.

Nonsubstantive Evidence

The arguments antagonists present are typically founded on little—or grossly misrepresented—evidence. As Shakespeare wrote in *Henry V,* "The empty vessel makes the greatest sound." With hollow evidence to back up their charges, antagonists nevertheless set up a huge clatter. Three common logical fallacies antagonists employ are *pettifogging* (quibbling over trifles, providing strong proof of irrelevant points); *extension* (exaggerating the opponent's position); and *argumentum ad ignorantium* (making an assertion that cannot be disproved and then claiming that the inability to disprove it makes it true).

Go Out of Their Way

Antagonists initiate trouble. They reach beyond—sometimes far beyond—their own areas of responsibility. They are often hypersensitive, taking every word and action as a personal attack and responding aggressively. A health care coordinator told me about a staff member who was preoccupied one morning and did not look up to greet a known antagonist. The antagonist followed the "offending" employee to her cubicle and loudly delivered a lecture on appropriate office etiquette. The antagonist then spent the next several weeks sabotaging every effort the staff member attempted. In desperation, she transferred to another department.

Insatiable Demands

Antagonists are never satisfied. The proverb "Give him an inch and he'll take a mile" applies doubly to antagonists. No amount of appeasement on your part (or on the part of a group or an organization as a whole) will ever suffice. Instead of calming them, attempts to placate antagonists only encourage them to make more demands. Many antagonists fight on until there is nothing left but rubble. Sometimes even that doesn't stop them.

Attacking

Harsh as the word *attacking* is, it accurately applies to antagonists. Although they may present some valid points, antagonists generally don't offer constructive criticism. Their implicit goal is control, no matter what the costs might be to others.

Selfish in Nature

The attacks of antagonists are self-serving. Often they will seize on a slogan or pick some side of a valid issue and pretend that is what they are fighting for. It rarely is. An antagonist will quickly drop a particular slogan or issue once it no longer serves his or her objectives.

Tearing Down Rather Than Building Up

The result of an antagonist's actions is people at odds with each other. Instead of bringing people together, antagonists divide them. Show me a divided and strife-torn group of people, large or small, and I would wager that one or more antagonists are in their midst.

Three Types of Antagonists

Antagonists are not a homogenous group. It is helpful to distinguish three types: hard-core antagonists, major antagonists, and moderate antagonists. Note that the dividing lines between these types are not as distinct as the process of categorization would make them appear.

Hard-Core Antagonists

Hard-core antagonists are seriously disturbed individuals. They are psychotic—out of touch with reality. Their psychosis is almost always of the paranoid variety, which by its nature is not as easy to detect as other psychoses. Many paranoid individuals can appear normal some or even most of the time. Hard-core antagonists tend to have incredible tenacity and an unbelievable desire to make trouble.

Major Antagonists

Major antagonists are not as severely disturbed as hard-core antagonists, yet they may exhibit similar behavior. The demands of major antagonists are similarly insatiable. Whereas you *cannot* reason with hard-core antagonists because they lack the emotional soundness to understand, major antagonists *will not* be reasoned with. They possess the capability of reasoning with those with whom they have issues, but they decline to exercise that capability.

Diagnostically, major antagonists have a character or personality disorder. They carry a great deal of hostility, coupled with an overwhelming drive for power. Although they are not psychotic or out of touch with reality, their personality problems are most certainly deep-seated. Major antagonists are not neurotic; neurotic individuals experience anxiety, possibly guilt, and feel dissatisfaction with their problems. They have a desire to change. Major antagonists do not.

Moderate Antagonists

Two features distinguish moderate antagonists from hard-core or major antagonists. First, moderate antagonists lack the self-starting quality of the others. If you were walking on one side of a street and antagonists of either of the first two types were on the other side, they would cross the street to give you trouble. Moderate antagonists would not go so far out of their way. If you both were walking on the same side of the street, however, the moderate antagonist would certainly take advantage of the opportunity to make trouble for you. In other words, an opportunity must be more closely available to moderate antagonists before they become actively antagonistic.

Part One: Identifying Antagonists

Second, moderate antagonists lack the tenacity of hard-core and major antagonists. Moderate antagonists have personality problems, but their problems are not as severe as those of either hard-core or major antagonists. They do make good followers of hard-core and major antagonists, though.

Not everyone who questions or criticizes is an antagonist; a person could be an *activist*. Activists do not fit into the definition of an antagonist, nor do they match any of the three types. The point is that you relate to activists and antagonists differently. While antagonists of all three types are malevolent in both intent and effect, activists are devoted to causes of some sort. They tend to stir the pot to try to effect change they believe will help. Even if you disagree with the substance of their cause, their intent is to try to bring about constructive change. Activists want action, no doubt, but they are *issue*-oriented, not *person*-oriented. Antagonists, on the other hand, are not out to effect constructive change, but to create dissension that benefits no one but the antagonist. They want attention, power, and control.

At times almost all of us are selfish or headstrong. Without excusing such behavior, you can be sure of this: Occasional surly behavior does not make an antagonist. What separates the rest of us from hard-core, major, and moderate antagonists is the ferociousness of the attacks and the insatiable or tenacious quality that drags out problems interminably.

CHAPTER **2**

Personality Characteristics of Antagonists

ONLY A SMALL PERCENTAGE OF PEOPLE ARE ANTAGO-NISTS, but the damage they cause is disproportionate to their numbers. It is essential for leaders to be able to distinguish true antagonists from those who are not.

With this in mind, here are some distinctive combinations of clustered personality characteristics and psychiatric syndromes that antagonists typically display.

General Personality Characteristics

Antagonists usually evidence several of five personality characteristics: negative self-concept, narcissism, aggression, rigidity, and authoritarianism. Although these same personality traits occur in "normal" individuals as well, antagonists exhibit them in extreme forms.

Negative Self-Concept

Self-image or self-concept is psychological shorthand for the feelings and thoughts, conscious and unconscious, that individuals have about themselves. Self-concept is an important factor in how people experience life. If one's self-concept is positive, society and other people tend to appear appealing, good, inviting, or benevolent. A positive self-concept opens the door to regarding others favorably, enables meaningful social interactions, and leads to productive behaviors. If one's self-concept is negative, the world appears frightening, angry, hostile, and threatening, often creating difficulty in properly understanding or relating to others. Someone with a negative self-concept frequently views the world with excessive pessimism.

Antagonists try to build themselves up by tearing others down. They express their inner struggles with a negative self-concept by attacking people, enjoying the failures and misfortunes of others, and assigning their own sense of worthlessness to others.

Narcissism

Narcissism is a personality pattern in which a person displays an excessive sense of self-importance and preoccupation with eliciting the admiration and attention of others. On the surface, a narcissistic individual seems to have an overabundance of positive self-concept, but appearances are deceiving. More often than not, narcissism disguises an inner sense of inadequacy. To compensate for these negative feelings, that is, to cover them up, a narcissistic individual greedily fishes for and hungrily devours the praise and attention of others. Yet attempting to hide feelings of inferiority and worthlessness in this way rarely works. The "praise-and-attention fix" lasts only a short time, and the individual is compelled to solicit renewed attention and admiration with the intensity and desperation of a chemically dependent person. Narcissistic people desperately need care, but unfortunately they are usually incapable of either receiving or benefiting from it.

Narcissistic people are usually oblivious to the rights and feelings of others, but other people may be slow to perceive them as being self-centered. Skilled in the art of deception, narcissistic persons are adept at appearing interested in others to win popularity. In reality, their efforts are focused on feeding their own egos, and they are unable to meet even the most basic needs of others. There is little authentic personal interaction; others are treated as a means for fulfilling their need for affirmation.

Narcissistic individuals who are also antagonists are extremely reluctant to admit wrongdoing. They cannot conceive of being in error because "right" is what meets their needs and "wrong" is what obstructs the meeting of those needs. According to these self-gratifying standards, the person chairing a meeting who denies an antagonist's purpose by stopping an uninvited tirade is judged by the antagonist as inherently wrong. Since antagonists define the world so that they are never wrong, others are always assumed to be at fault.

Aggression

Antagonists display patterns of aggressive behavior that permeate their entire personalities. Angry at self, the world, and any convenient situation or person, antagonists wander through life seeking, inviting, and collecting injustices against themselves. Every wrong, actual or perceived, is stored in their memories and periodically replayed to supply fuel for their anger.

Everyone has aggressive feelings at times, but for antagonists, aggression is a way of life. They tend to legitimize their abusive outbursts by projecting those feelings onto others, convincing themselves that others are treating them unfairly. In that way, antagonists easily justify their aggressive actions in their own minds.

Not all aggression manifests itself in physical or verbal activity. In fact, passive aggression can be every bit as malicious as active aggression. Characterized by procrastination and constant inefficiency, passive aggression is tailor-made to frustrate others. Typically, there is no overt opposition from the individual, such as a blatant refusal to comply with instructions. Rather, there is an apparently cooperative attitude but no resulting action.

A passive-aggressive antagonist undertaking an assignment for a supervisor will have plenty of excuses, but won't have the work in hand when the deadline arrives. Using all available means, the passive-aggressive person sets roadblock after roadblock in silent acts of hostility.

Rigidity

When emotional and personal growth stops too soon, rigidity is one result. Rigidity is characterized by inflexibility of thought, usually coupled with excessive concern for precise and accurate procedure (as defined by the rigid individual). Those with rigid personalities see the world as totally static; their explanation of events is, by definition, the unquestionably correct interpretation. Rigid individuals sometimes ridicule or ignore differing opinions and willfully overlook or skillfully obscure contrary evidence. Attempting to create a sense of security in an apparently unstable, frightening world, those with rigid personality structures are devoted to keeping their narrow views intact.

It is important to note that people who are not antagonists can have rigid personalities, too. But when antagonists have rigid personality structures, the effects are magnified. Antagonists with rigid personality structures are more prone to antagonistic behaviors for two reasons: (1) Their feelings of peace, security, and harmony are heavily dependent on the integrity of their worldview. When it becomes impossible for them to ignore dissent, they strike out against those who threaten to topple their systems. (2) They are especially jealous of leaders, because people in authority have the power to disrupt their narrow world, to interfere with what they need to feel secure. Therefore, rigid antagonists frequently employ their narrow rules and regulations as weapons against leaders.

Authoritarianism

Authoritarian individuals are characterized by two seemingly contradictory drives: (1) the need to admire and submit to those they consider "powerful," and (2) the need to be in authority and make others submit to them. Individuals with authoritarian tendencies divide the world into two camps: those who are strong and those who are weak. Whatever is characterized as strong elicits the authoritarian's veneration (usually involving a combination of fear and admiration) and a desire to submit to the stronger object. Whatever is characterized as weak arouses a desire to dominate, attack, and humiliate or annihilate the weaker object.

When antagonists view the world through authoritarian eyes, the consequences are even more significant. Because antagonists are less likely to attack those whom they perceive as strong, it is vital to communicate strength to them (the subject of chapters 8, 10, 13, and 18). Also, when a strong system of mutual support is established among leaders (the subject of chapters 11-12), antagonists lose the fissures and fracture points that enable them to create disunity in the department or organization.

Psychiatric Syndromes

In addition to showing an excess of the preceding personality characteristics, antagonists commonly possess one or both of two clinical syndromes: paranoid personality and antisocial personality. Any of the five general personality characteristics can combine with either one or both of these syndromes.

Paranoid Personality

Paranoid-related attitudes and activities encompass a wide range—from minor suspicion present in everyone at one time or another to severe paranoid schizophrenia found in a small percentage of individuals. Most antagonists fall into the middle and upper portions of the paranoid spectrum. Marks of a paranoid personality include persistent, unwarranted guardedness and mistrust of others; delusions of grandeur; lack of genuine emotions; and hypersensitivity. Negative experiences in early childhood often make these individuals very sensitive to the smallest traces of hostility, contempt, criticism, or accusation in the attitudes of others. This hypersensitivity will always find something or someone on which to feed. Because they distrust others, paranoid persons try to find hidden meanings in words and actions, continually looking for ulterior motives behind what others say.

Many paranoid persons are capable of functioning in society, maintaining contact with reality except in areas bordering on their delusions. Despite their adequate handling of daily activities, they commonly experience difficulty in relating to others; disagreements and arguments are commonplace. Paranoid individuals find authority figures, in particular, most difficult to get along with.

Because of their suspiciousness, paranoid persons rarely seek counseling or psychotherapy. Furthermore, they would interpret a gentle and well-meant suggestion to seek professional help as a personal attack, serving only to validate the notion that others are out to get them. When they are forced to obtain therapeutic help, results are usually negligible. Convinced that the therapist is in collaboration with others against them, paranoid individuals usually cannot trust the therapist sufficiently to open up and receive help.

This fear of seeking outside help doesn't apply only to mental health professionals. One person in a state social services department told me about a conflict with a peer that had somehow escalated significantly. He suggested bringing in professional mediation to reach a compromise. In a voice dripping with scorn, the antagonist said, "You'll do anything to get your own way, won't you," and stalked toward the meeting room door. As a parting shot, he turned and said, "If you will tell lies before this group, what's to stop you from telling lies to a mediator?"

Along with delusions of persecution, paranoid antagonists also have delusions of grandeur, seeing themselves as the

Part One: Identifying Antagonists

center of attention. This makes it easy for them to believe that others—especially those in leadership positions—are plotting against them.

Paranoid individuals often project their own feelings onto others. Attributing their own feelings to others—projection—is a means to avoid taking responsibility for their own feelings and actions. Those who feel threatened by their own unacceptable ideas, feelings, or shortcomings will try to protect their self-image by attributing these feelings to others instead of themselves. For example, if an antagonist is dishonest in the workplace, he or she may accuse a supervisor or other leader of being dishonest—or lazy or "not liking people," whatever the antagonist's own problem may be.

A supervisor or manager is often tempted to try to convince a paranoid antagonist that his or her delusions are false, but any attempt at reasoning is quite fruitless. It is precisely at that point where the individual pushes reality aside. When a nonparanoid individual is similarly engaged in rational discussion, he or she would be more likely to say, "I guess I have been acting foolishly." Not so with the paranoid antagonist, who is convinced that the supervisor is clearly demonstrating that he or she is out to get the antagonist, doesn't understand, or has been misled by others.

One disconcerting aspect of the paranoid delusional system is the kernel of truth it inevitably contains, but this should not be so surprising. Just as it is impossible for any leader to be 100% right, it is similarly difficult for a paranoid antagonist to be 100% wrong. The danger becomes apparent when a paranoid antagonist is able to convince others that his or her whole delusion is accurate because a small bit is based on reality.

Antisocial Personality

Besides classic paranoia, antagonists often exhibit a second psychiatric syndrome—antisocial personality (alternatively known as psychopathy or sociopathy). People with antisocial personalities suffer from a significant lack of moral development, accompanied by an inability to live within the limits of socially acceptable behavior.

As a result of inadequately developed consciences, antagonists with antisocial personalities experience little guilt or anxiety about the pain they inflict on others. The antisocial antagonist's actions appear cruel to others, but he or she is incapable of fully understanding the moral concept of *cruelty*.

Antisocial antagonists are usually very likable, especially at first. They are often bright, spontaneous, and adept at putting up a good front in order to obtain the admiration and support of others. Their extreme likability enables them to put others at ease almost effortlessly. But they are also manipulative and guileful, treating others as objects for accomplishing their own ends. They have difficulty maintaining in-depth relationships. While they may appear to be popular, having many acquaintances, they have no intimate friends. Their emotions are shallow and rarely shared with others—or even acknowledged by themselves.

When finally confronted with their own unacceptable behavior, antisocial antagonists might ardently promise to change. Indeed they might seem to change—for a while. But then the same behavior will reappear. Like the paranoid personality, an antisocial personality is highly resistant to change. Discomfort moves the average person to seek help, but an antisocial individual experiences no discomfort. The only anxiety

Part One: Identifying Antagonists

sociopaths suffer is the fear of being unable to achieve their purposes or of getting caught.

After reading this chapter, you may be concerned that you have identified some antagonistic characteristics in yourself. Relax. All of us, from time to time, may display some of these traits. What distinguishes antagonists from the rest of us is degree. Antagonists not only possess a good number of these characteristics, but the characteristics dominate their personalities.

> Note: While a common, and almost inevitable, characteristic of a true antagonist is that he or she will have a psychological disorder, it is important that you do not deal with antagonists in the workplace based upon a bias or perception that such an employee labors under a mental disability or mental illness. Taking employment actions against an employee because you regard them as mentally disabled or perceive them to have a mental disability can be actionable under the Americans with Disabilities Act and any number of state Human Rights Acts. Your organization should only deal with the antagonists' *actions* and *conduct* and not engage in speculation or supposition about the nature of any deep-seated psychological basis for the behavior.

CHAPTER **3**

Red Flags of Antagonism

Antagonists typically walk around displaying "red flags" that say to those who recognize them, "I'm an antagonist and proud of it!" This chapter identifies red flags that antagonists display even before they commence an attack.

After you finish this chapter, you may find yourself looking suspiciously at your coworkers, neighbors, and friends. In your eagerness you may think you see antagonists under every rock and behind every tree. That's all right: Your initial, excessive suspicion will pass in due time, and you will be left with what Karl Menninger called *healthy paranoia,* an attitude enabling you to be on your guard without being guarded, to defend yourself without being defensive.

Antagonists rarely wave only one flag. Usually an antagonist displays several—often half a dozen or more. Not all flags proclaim with equal clarity, "I am an antagonist." Some flags announce, "I might be an antagonist *if* you see more flags in my hand." Antagonists typically identify themselves clearly, though, and do so early. Just pay attention to the signals.

You may react to what you read by listing exceptions you know: "So-and-so does that, but he's not an antagonist." Or perhaps, "I do that, and I'm not an antagonist." There are exceptions, of course. Still, as the park ranger warned the city slicker, "If you see a small black animal with a white stripe and bushy tail, don't pet it." The presence of one or more red flags does not guarantee that you are dealing with an antagonist, but it will give you fair warning to exercise caution.

What follows is a review, in descending order of severity, of eighteen red flags antagonists often display even before they go on the offensive in organizations.

The Previous Track Record Flag

Some antagonists will in effect wave a red flag announcing: "See how antagonistically I behaved before!" They could have played the role of antagonist earlier in the present organization, or they might have done so somewhere else. One upper-level manager described this to me as the "broken glass trail." She could track antagonists by following the trail of broken glass. Wherever antagonists went, she found herself sweeping up the broken glass of previous conflicts. It was a chronic symptom, she said, not just limited to specific topics, audiences, or relationships.

In talking with another manager about an antagonist, I asked if he knew whether the individual had behaved antagonistically in other settings or with previous employers. He sighed and nodded his head, saying, "It's like he's a serial killer."

Don't ignore this clear signal or think, "It won't happen to me." Those with antagonistic track records tend not to change.

The Parallel Track Record Flag

Individuals who behave antagonistically in other arenas of life are prime candidates to become active antagonists in your organization. These persons may not currently be acting antagonistically at work but are behaving this way in one or more other situations, such as school board meetings or in a social club. The antagonist may even brag about these behaviors. In so doing, the individual conspicuously waves a red flag before you. You might expect these people to keep silent about their antagonism for fear of being detected, but antagonists have a kind of bravado about this. Their grandiose view of themselves causes them to believe that everyone will wholeheartedly support their activities—indeed, they are convinced that no one could possibly disagree with them.

The Nameless Others Flag

All leaders, whatever their position, receive criticism from time to time. Sometimes the criticism is valid, helpful, and legitimate. Even when the criticism is not valid, it can still indicate a healthy relationship in process—a sign of trust from the one doing the criticizing.

When someone offers you a word of criticism, however, and adds, "There are X number of other people who feel the same way," chances are excellent that you are talking with an antagonist. These "others" may be phantoms of the antagonist's imagination, invented to validate his or her own feelings and to threaten you. Or they may be followers of the antagonist. Whether or not they exist is immaterial because individuals who are not antagonists don't need to talk about "all the others" who feel

Part One: Identifying Antagonists

the same way; they simply express their own thoughts and feelings.

One test to determine whether someone is or is not an antagonist in this situation is to respond casually, "Oh, I'm sorry to hear that. Who are these other people?" If the person lists a few names, you may not be faced with an antagonist. An antagonist is more likely to answer: "I can't tell you. They came to me in the strictest of confidence."

The Predecessor Put-Down Flag

Beware of those who denounce your predecessor and praise you in the same breath. They might say something like, "You're my kind of supervisor, a person I can relate to—not like the others." In certain ways, everyone enjoys hearing words like these. Leaders can be seduced by such compliments, but a person criticizing one or more others and simultaneously flattering you carries a flag of blazing scarlet. Someday you may be the former supervisor, and those who build up the new supervisor will do so at your expense.

The Instant Buddy Flag

Be cautious with those who relate to you in an overly friendly fashion as soon as you begin a new job or immediately after they transfer into your area. When you first arrive, these individuals will be all too ready to pull you aside, offering to "give you the real lowdown on what it's all about here." They will characteristically spend much time and effort probing you and trying to become intimately acquainted. Later, however, their inquisitiveness will turn to the proverbial cool contempt bred of familiarity.

If you have the feeling someone is presuming intimacy with you too quickly, beware. One key feature that distinguishes those likely to be antagonists from others who may be genuinely friendly or hospitable is that the antagonist will begin to tear down and criticize others very soon. Often this destructive criticism will begin in your first encounter.

The Gushing Praise Flag

Have you ever had someone heap excessive praise on you? That kind of positive reinforcement is nice, isn't it? But those who lavish effusive, gushing praise on you now will often be equally generous with their criticism later.

What causes this shift? One possibility may be unrealistic expectations. To be human is to have faults. You cannot sustain the level of perfection that antagonists expect. It is also possible that they become jealous of the image they have built up for you and consequently seek to destroy it by bringing you down to their size. In any case, beware of someone who heaps excessive praise on you. This person is waving a red flag.

The "I Gotcha" Flag

Beware of those who try to catch you in error—for example, those who publicly ask you questions to which you know they already know the answers. Imagine you have just finished making a presentation suggesting a creative innovation. Someone who has antagonistic tendencies might ask, knowing the answer full well, "Before you came to this job, did you work in this area, or is your experience in some other area?" This kind of question is mere subterfuge—an obvious attempt to try to force you into a defensive response. To embarrass you before a group of your peers or superiors, the antagonist might also ask tough questions that would be hard to answer without preparation. Or the person might let an error in a report go unremarked when you send it out for previews, but point it out during an important meeting. In other instances, the antagonist will be the one to call attention to some little glitch or flaw in an otherwise well-executed job. The aim is to cast suspicion on all you have done. Those who display such behavior offer public warnings that they may be antagonists.

The Extraordinary Likability Flag

I'm sure you have already met an individual like this—the kind of person you immediately like, enjoy, and feel comfortable around, someone so disarmingly charming that he or she gives you no reason to withhold anything in a relationship. Someone like this, who exudes only smoothness and perfection, might be an antagonist.

Surprising? Very. But true nonetheless. Beware of overly smooth individuals who seem to have no foibles. To be sure, other red flags need to be present before one can be confident of such an individual's antagonistic leanings, but be vigilant. As a friend of mine says, "There are two kinds of people who are charming: those who are really charming—and serial killers."

The Job-Hopper Flag

Beware of those who constantly jump from job to job. Not everyone who changes jobs frequently is an antagonist, but this is simply one of the flags to keep an eye on. Antagonists change jobs because they are dissatisfied with the position, the supervisor, or the outcome of a decision in the previous company—and they will tell you so! Indeed, they often confide that they have been dissatisfied with almost every supervisor or manager with whom they were previously associated. At the same time, job-hoppers will build you up. "Finally," they exclaim, "I have found the boss for me!" If they are indeed antagonists and you permit them to run roughshod over you, they could be right. You *are* just what they're looking for.

The Liar Flag

Beware of individuals who lie. Their lying need not be specifically associated with antagonistic activity; however, people who lie—about anything—are more likely to be antagonistic than those who don't. The lie might involve something quite harmless, such as a small detail about where the person went to school or whether he or she had a particular responsibility with a former employer. Some would say that exaggeration on résumés is to be expected since a résumé is obviously intended to extol one's virtues. But there's a difference between making oneself look good and lying. A person who fabricates a past is not just omitting history; he or she is rewriting it.

Sometimes liars operate as misquoters. They are likely to say, "But you said . . ." and then feed back something similar to what you said, but with a twist. The twist always benefits the antagonist, either by making you look bad or in some way building up the antagonist.

The Aggressive Means Flag

You can sometimes recognize antagonists by the means they propose or employ to accomplish their ends. Antagonists tend to use methods that are extreme, unethical, combative, and insensitive, or any combination of these. Vicious language that impugns the character of another is a mark of an antagonist; careful, reasoned assertions concerning another person's stance on an issue is the mark of someone seeking to find a solution.

"Aha!" you might say. "Then any pushy sales representative might be an antagonist." No, it's not as simple as that. Is the person in question willing to hurt others, destroy their reputations, vandalize someone's files or other property? If so, you can safely assess the behavior as aggressive means and the person as a likely antagonist.

The Note-Taker Flag

Be wary of those who take notes at inappropriate times—such as during a conversation when an off-the-cuff opinion is expressed on a sensitive issue. Inappropriate note takers often are budding antagonists.

The Flesh-Tearing Flag

"Flesh-tearing" is a literal translation of the Greek roots for the word *sarcasm*. This flag describes someone who uses sharp, cutting language such as sarcasm or a barbed comment disguised as a joke. An individual who consistently uses sarcasm is a viable candidate for the position of antagonist. "Tearing down" is the key element to remember from the definition of an antagonist. This is not about good-natured banter, repartee, or clever retorts. It's about downright nastiness. Antagonists use sarcasm to rend as much flesh as they can.

The Different Drummer Flag

Beware of those who conspicuously and consistently resist established policies, insisting on doing things their own way. A "different drummer" makes these changes without consultation and often by surprise, even bragging, "I've never played by the rules; I've never been a good soldier." Such a person feels compelled to march to the beat of his or her own drum.

A certain degree of free thinking is healthy, and many people with these characteristics are in no way antagonistic. The important distinction to make is between those who build up the organization and those whose actions tear it down. Antagonists follow only the rule of expediency: "Rules are good for others, not for me." Their attitude is characterized more by conniving than by contriving, and they can play havoc with the orderly conduct of an organization's life. This flag needs to be considered in combination with the others.

The Pest Flag

A "pest" may be an insatiable questioner, a persistent suggester, or an incessant drop-in visitor to your office. Another possible signal of this flag is a continuous flurry of communications, often about picky details. This is a less significant red flag; many pesky persons are not antagonists but simply well-intentioned individuals who end up being nuisances. Occasionally, however, such behavior may be the tip of the iceberg—a fairly innocent behavior that results from an antagonistic personality. People who first appear to be simply pests may later prove to be thoroughgoing antagonists, but only consider this flag along with the presence of others.

The Situational Loser Flag

Every organization makes decisions, and decisions create sides. When a conflict requires a decision, some win and others lose. While disagreements and conflicts can provide occasions for growth, some people take losses very poorly. For them, being on the losing end of an issue precipitates antagonistic behavior.

You may want to pay a bit more attention to employees who lose on a particular issue. This red flag is only significant when it appears with other flags.

The Cause Flag

Philipp Melanchthon, a 16th-century scholar, once said, "Nothing can be stated so perfectly as not to be misunderstood." It is for that reason that I hesitate to include this red flag, but its relevance warrants it.

I am very thankful for the individuals throughout history who have promoted causes and helped to right some of the world's great wrongs. Nonetheless, there appears to be a correlation between individuals who promote causes and those who behave antagonistically. Obviously not everyone who supports a cause should be branded an antagonist, and therefore this flag should attract much less attention than the others. One associated flag you might want to look for is how far someone will go to promote a cause (see the Aggressive Means Flag, page 38).

Also, be on the lookout for escalating demands related to the cause—the insatiable quality of antagonists may betray their presence, making you realize that the individual you're dealing with really is not interested in a solution to whatever the issue is but in garnering power.

The School of Hard Knocks Flag

Successful people with little formal education or those who have struggled against great adversity to succeed are often called "graduates of the school of hard knocks." Most graduates of this "school" are not antagonists. It is nevertheless startling to note how many antagonists have had to fight their way up. Further, antagonists are particularly apt to flaunt their struggle. They seem compelled to brag about it as though it somehow validates their actions. Not every person coming up the hard way is an antagonist, but be cautious when you spot this red flag along with others.

Avoid making any snap judgments about individuals. But do remember that, for the sake of your organization and the individuals in it, discernment is necessary. Individuals who wave these red flags merit closer scrutiny. After some consideration, you may relax, or you may decide to pay closer attention. Knowing these indicators—and knowing them well—is worth every bit of time you give it.

> Note: While these flags are valuable in identifying antagonists, all are based upon observed antagonistic behavior. Be careful to scrutinize and react to *behavior* and not to stereotype or bias. Taking adverse action

without sound foundation in real behavior may open the organization to possible liability under employment discrimination laws. Ensure that the "flag" is a behavior indicator, not discriminatory bias.

CHAPTER **4**

Recognizing the Tactics and Maneuvers of Antagonists

If I were writing a book on how to deal with vampires, I would include a section on the red flags they display—wearing black capes, arriving with eerie music, having sinister voices, and avoiding mirrors.

But at the ball in a castle in Transylvania, just knowing a vampire on sight isn't enough. On their best party behavior, vampires can be rather charming—just like antagonists. You would need to know the signs of an impending attack.

If someone who is not a vampire were staring at your neck, you might find such attention to be embarrassing or unwelcome, but you would not consider it dangerous. If a known vampire takes an interest in your neck, however, it is time to sharpen up the old wooden stake, get out the garlic, and don your shiniest silver cross.

Just as you can recognize the red flags that antagonists wave, you can also discern the tactics and strategies that they may use—both in early skirmishes and in full-blown assaults—so that you can take the appropriate action to prevent or minimize the damage.

Before you sound the alarm, however, you need to satisfy yourself with regard to two conditions:

- Antagonistic behaviors are indeed present.
- They are coming from a person who has been waving red flags.

If both conditions exist, an attack is under way, and you and others need to respond appropriately. If either condition fails your test, you can probably relax. But take one more look to make sure you didn't miss any red flags.

Early Tactics

By alerting yourself to the earliest stages of an antagonist's attack, you gain a distinct advantage. You can minimize the damage done by dealing effectively with the individual before major problems erupt. Early intervention is easier to manage. To this end, consider these early tactics an antagonist might employ.

A Chill in the Relationship

When a person who is evidencing red flags changes his or her manner of relating to you, beware. This could be an initial sign of an antagonistic attack. Where once he or she might have been warm and cordial, now there is icy coldness and perhaps blatant rudeness. When you greet the antagonist in passing, he or she might respond coldly or not at all. He or she might avoid being alone with you—perhaps feeling uneasy about his or her intentions or as a manipulative ploy to upset you.

In group situations the antagonist might show disrespect toward you, use biting sarcasm even over trivial matters, or display a condescending attitude. For example, he or she might make a point of mispronouncing your name to irritate you. The underlying intent of these manipulations is to give the antagonist the upper hand and discredit you in front of others.

Honeyed "Concerns"

As an antagonist begins activity, he or she might pay you a visit or send you a letter of "concern." *I have a concern* can be an antagonist's way of saying, "I am very angry." Of course, anger can be appropriate and healthy. Both antagonists and nonantagonists get angry because this is part of being human. But a red-flag person who expresses pseudoconcern is simply masking his or her anger with surface politeness. Consider the visit or letter as only the first move. More will follow—how much more depends on your response to these initial moves.

Irritating Questions

A red-flag person might begin by asking a number of picky questions, checking out minor details like: "Where do we buy our coffee for the lunchroom coffeepot?" or "How many times did your department meet all together last year?"—even though this is outside his or her area of responsibility. You find yourself feeling upset and exasperated as the antagonist becomes a constant irritant.

Mobilizing Forces and Pot-Stirring

To wage an effective campaign, an antagonist must gather support and create discord, conflict, and doubt. He or she might try any number of approaches to accomplish this end. The behavior could be as innocuous as whispering to others nearby during a meeting or as serious as flooding the organization or

Part One: Identifying Antagonists

department with rumors—not the ordinary kind that plague all organizations, but destructive, insinuating gossip strategically directed against key people.

The antagonist also thrives on unofficial backroom meetings. You may notice the antagonist forming impromptu cluster meetings at break or lunchtimes, before or after a meeting. Realize that nonantagonists simply don't behave this way. If they have a concern, they will either appropriately share their ideas during a meeting or speak directly to you at some other time.

E-mail is a prime instrument for pot stirring and mobilizing forces. One antagonist sent this e-mail to a coworker: "You looked so down this morning when I came in. Are you okay?" The person responded, "Yes, I just had a project returned to me to be revised, and I'm feeling overwhelmed." Back came the reply: "Don't they give us too much work, though. . . ." The antagonist was sowing discord and trying to recruit a follower at the same time!

Another particularly effective version of this tactic, at least from the antagonist's perspective, is the reply-to-all e-mail. This approach can sow discord in a wholesale fashion, triggering a disruptive series of attacks, defensive replies, and rebuttals.

The telephone is another ready tool: the antagonist is "calling just to check some things out" or has some "serious concerns about the company" or about a particular supervisor or another individual and wants to see if anyone else is worried. As a result, others could indeed become critical of certain leaders, influenced by the antagonist's insinuations and lies.

Meddling

Antagonists often use the tactic of meddling in areas that are not their concern. If a red-flag person abruptly shows an unusual interest in another work area, he or she has probably sniffed out a vulnerable weakness. Such meddling is cause for alarm.

Another way of meddling is by constantly bringing complaints against coworkers or other supervisors. Antagonists are nitpickers and are often relentless with complaints. One leader told me he can pick out an antagonist by the way he or she uses and abuses the organizational grievance and complaint systems by filing multiple charges against managers, most of which turn out to be without merit.

Open and accessible internal dispute resolution processes are vital management tools and, in some instances, are necessary for an organization to properly protect itself in legal disputes. Be careful not to impair access or utility of these processes because of the perception that an antagonist might abuse the system. A properly run complaint system should address bad faith, groundless, and abusive complaints.

Resistance

Finally, you might detect growing resistance and independence from a red-flag person. Resistance might be active, taking the form of openly ridiculing the management of the organization, defying your authority as manager or supervisor, or blocking the approval of certain matters that ordinarily glide through the administrative machinery with ease. On the other hand, antagonists might exhibit passive resistance such as withdrawing from an activity while making a public issue of it—

emphasizing that his or her nonparticipation is connected with the "concerns" he or she is expressing about the organization. Antagonists are typically not content to disappear quietly. Usually they let others know loud and clear that they are absent and why.

Later Tactics

Antagonists are not stamped from the same mold; there are probably as many antagonistic behaviors as there are antagonists. Nevertheless, from the diversity of their behaviors certain patterns emerge. A partial list follows, describing typical behaviors of antagonists when their attacks are already well along. Not every antagonist will display all these behaviors; some might evidence three or four of them without displaying any others. In any case, if you encounter an active antagonist, you will witness at least some of these characteristic behaviors.

Sloganeering

Antagonists often use one or more emotionally laden slogans to spread troublesome dissension. For example:

> "Washington is a good man, but not good for this organization."
>
> "It may seem like Al knows what he's doing, but he really doesn't."
>
> "Emma shoots first, then thinks."
>
> "Meghan hogs all the credit."
>
> "Luis is trying to poison our minds."
>
> "Janice spends the company's money like there's no tomorrow."

Slogans of this kind are hit-and-run incidents. There is no constructive purpose to them. Antagonists may also make statements like these in a jovial manner with a big smile—hiding behind humor to do their damage.

Accusing

Antagonists frequently bandy about one or more accusations. You might hear:

> "No one in your unit respects you."
>
> "You don't really know what is going on here, but I do."
>
> "You never listen."
>
> "You never follow through."
>
> "You micromanage."
>
> "You make changes too fast/too slow."
>
> "You don't trust me."

And on and on. The antagonist's theory (and it works!) is, if you say something often enough, it begins to take on a life of its own. Accusations such as these often project onto the accused what the accuser consciously or unconsciously feels about him- or herself.

Accusing by insinuation and innuendo is another ploy. "Don's a pretty good engineer, but don't ever play golf with him." You're left wondering: Is Don a cheat? A very good golfer? A very bad golfer? If you ask, "Why?" the antagonist is likely to respond, "You'll find out when you play with him."

Spying

In more or less obvious ways, an antagonist may begin to spy on you. He or she might telephone to see where you are or even follow you. The antagonist may keep a log of your times in and out, your time on the phone, for example—anything and everything you do. He or she might go through your trash to try and find something to use against you.

Research turned up a number of stories about antagonists rummaging through outboxes or desks or opening someone else's mail and making copies for their own purposes. One manager walked into his office early one morning to find a known antagonist rifling through his files. The man just smirked a little, calmly shut the drawer, and left the office. Even though the manager immediately had the locks changed on the cabinets, he said he never again felt beyond the antagonist's reach.

The lengths to which an antagonist will go to spy on someone are illustrated by this story a company president related to me. He and some others from the company went a couple of times a week after work to an outdoor tennis court in one of the city's parks. A man who was later determined to be an antagonist would show up, without fail, to watch for the entire time they played tennis. The next day the antagonist would tell others in the office how the president had cheated or made "cheap shots" during the game.

Recording conversations is another favorite method of antagonists. One supervisor discovered an employee who secretly taped all of their conversations on a minirecorder in her pocket. Others record phone conversations. A wise rule: Be as noncommittal as possible when talking in person or on the phone with a known antagonist.

Recognizing Tactics and Maneuvers

Distorting

Antagonists may save your communications to quote out of context, misquote, or otherwise use against you. They also frequently distort reports of incidents, leaving just enough grains of truth to maintain credibility. For example, if the owner of a business became slightly vexed during the course of a meeting, an antagonist might say: "Did you see how she blew up! Lack of control like that casts a cloud over the entire meeting! I worry about this company sometimes."

Smirking

Body language

A troublemaker might wear an inappropriate smile or a cocky grin when he or she encounters the person under attack. Such a smirk says, "I've got you on the run." Smirks and other mean-spirited facial expressions may take place in meetings, too. It is infuriating but will gratify the antagonist more if you allow an antagonist's smirk to obviously get to you.

Pestering

Antagonists sometimes pester managers or other leaders by flooding them with e-mails, constantly calling on the phone, or by hanging around after work or a meeting, saying, "I'd like a brief word with you." Obsessed with a particular issue, they may come to a leader's office multiple times within several days with more information or comments about the same or a closely related topic.

One manager told me about the ways in which an antagonist tenaciously pestered him: "The antagonist showed up for work at exactly the same time I did to 'walk in with me.' He joined me in the cafeteria for lunch to 'bend my ear.' He hung around the department, monopolizing the secretaries' time, in order to catch me going in or out of my office. But I finally had to do something about it when he started following me into the restroom to 'continue our little chat' there!"

I agree, you might say, that pestering is an annoyance, but is it really a tactic in an antagonist's arsenal? Definitely. Pestering can be a tool to gain information to use against you simply because, with the antagonist's unending presence, he or she might be able to catch you off guard. More importantly, the antagonist is stealing from you the one thing you can never replace: your time.

Constant pestering underscores the tenacious character of an antagonist.

Copiously Communicating

Antagonists frequently barrage leaders with e-mails, memos, or even letters. Acknowledge these at first—perhaps with a very brief phone call or by sending a response such as this:

> Dear _____:
>
> Thank you for your concern. I appreciate responsible feedback.
>
> (Signed or initialed)

One of the most counterproductive courses of action would be to respond at length in a long letter, for example, refuting the antagonist's accusations point by point. A letter of rebuttal does absolutely no good, serving only to add fuel to the antagonist's fire rather than quenching it.

Here is a fundamental assumption about antagonists that you should apply as a guiding principle in dealing with them: *Normal ways of dealing with conflict and criticism not only do not work with antagonists but actually make things worse.* Once you make this adjustment in your thinking, much of the battle is won.

Pretense

Antagonists often portray themselves as champions of the underdog or as underdogs themselves. The sociological impact of that pretense is usually quite significant. People cheer for the underdog and for those who seem to be championing the underdog. One manager told me about an antagonist who would sanctimoniously preface a blistering attack by saying, "I'm only trying to protect the people in this organization."

Lobbying

Antagonists frequently lobby particular groups within an organization to create doubt about one or more leaders. Lobbying almost always takes place secretly or behind the scenes. New employees, in particular, are a very vulnerable group that antagonists try to lobby.

An elementary teacher told me about her experience with a person she now knows was an antagonist:

> I began to notice that "P" was always quick to befriend new teachers. She was the first to meet them and graciously offer assistance. Very soon, however, she would begin raising doubts in their minds about the administration's policies and procedures. She usually managed to get the new teachers to do the "dirty

work" of confronting administrators with concerns and problems. Many of these nontenured teachers were not rehired the next year because they were seen as troublemakers, while the driving force behind them—the actual antagonist—was not dealt with at all.

Since lobbying is not necessarily a highly conspicuous activity, antagonists can use the guise of friendship to carry out their divisive tactics while keeping above the fray.

Sources of Information

Knowledge about an antagonist's tactics or maneuvers is helpful, but you may still be wondering how you can gather the information you need in order to tell whether or not you are under attack.

First and foremost, keep your eyes and ears open. Be aware of what is happening around you. If you know the 18 red flags that antagonists wave, listed in chapter 3, and if you can recognize when someone is waving one or more flags, you have a major advantage.

Second, pay attention to the observations of mature, trusted colleagues and supervisors. When people you trust and respect make assertions about those whom you might have already recognized as red-flag wavers, you would be well-advised to consider what they say. One manager who was forewarned told me, "I was put on alert to be careful by my two prior supervisors. They both said, 'She will keep you spinning in circles, and essentially you won't be able to make the simplest decision because you will become paralyzed with self-doubt about your abilities.'"

Third, you might also want to ask other people questions about the individual you think might be an antagonist. But take care how you do this. Your questions should focus on work- and task-related behavior. Make sure you remain professional and keep emotions out of the process. You need to be extremely sensitive in choosing the time, place, occasion, and person to question. Don't actively seek this information at the lower levels of your organization, but rather seek such information at the level to which you belong and from those who are above you in the organization. If possible, ask your predecessor. Go ahead and ask, but be discreet.

Finally, trust your sixth sense. Sometimes you sense that something is wrong—a vague uneasiness that a certain individual cannot be trusted. Don't become overly suspicious, but at the same time, grant your sixth sense a fair hearing.

Whatever you do, keep your eyes and ears open. Don't close your eyes and hope that what you don't like will go away. It won't.

CHAPTER 5

Levels of Organizational Conflict

CONFLICT IS A FACT OF LIFE. Conflict that hones the edge of an organization and keeps it mindful of and true to its purposes is healthy. An organization with no conflict (and I don't know of any) must either have no purpose or, at best, a very frivolous purpose.

Conflict itself is not necessarily a problem and is not the subject of this book. On a values scale, conflict is neutral. It can be good or bad, healthy or unhealthy, creative or destructive. Antagonism makes up only a small percentage of the wide range of conflict that exists in organizations because only a small percentage of an organization's employees are antagonists. Antagonism is bad, unhealthy, and destructive.

Some specialists in the field of conflict resolution are discovering that they have treated conflict too narrowly. Too often it was assumed that all parties involved in conflicts were mentally healthy, morally responsible, rational, and willing to compromise. Experience has shown that such assumptions, while applying to the great majority of individuals, overlook a very notable, vocal, and disruptive minority. The result has been to

Part One: Identifying Antagonists

equip mentally sound and morally responsible individuals to work through healthy conflict with other mentally sound and morally responsible people, but to leave them at a loss when confronted with antagonists.

Literature in the area of conflict resolution recognizes that there are individuals who initiate and thrive on unhealthy conflict, persons who have no desire whatsoever to see conflict resolved. Author Speed Leas has noted that much of the existing literature on conflict does little to help people determine the severity of conflict and adjust their responses accordingly.[1] In answer to this need, Leas distinguished five levels of conflict (see Figure 1).

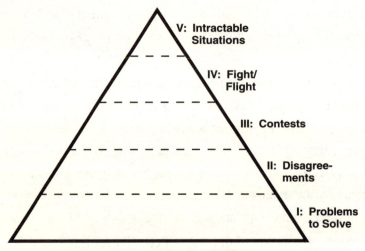

Figure 1: Levels of Conflict

According to Leas, what differentiates the various levels are the objectives of those involved and the language they use.

---

[1] Speed Leas, *Moving Your Church Through Conflict*, Washington, D.C.: The Alban Institute, 1985. Used by permission.

The objective of those operating at Level I, *Problems to Solve,* is to work out a solution to the problem, whatever it is. Anger may surface (as on any level), but the focus remains on finding an amicable resolution to the conflict. Those operating at this level do not perceive the conflict as person-oriented. They make full use of rational opportunities to work out a solution, and their communication is quite open. Individuals operating on this level use language that is straightforward and centered in the here and now. They have no hidden agendas.

At Level II, *Disagreements,* the objective becomes colored with a need for self-protection. There is a shift from unreserved openness to some guardedness, shrewdness, and calculation—not actually hostile, except perhaps in the manifestation of some unkind humor or biting criticism in the language used. At this level, individuals move away from dealing with specifics and tend toward generalizations. Those operating at Level II frequently turn to compromise as their method of dealing with differences.

Those operating at Level III, *Contests,* view conflict from a "win/lose" perspective. The objective is no longer to solve the problem. Even self-protection has faded into the background. What matters is winning, putting one's opponents "in their proper place." The language used by those operating on this level reveals some perceptual distortion. Although it occurs less frequently, it is still possible to achieve healthy resolution of conflict at this level.

Parties operating at Level IV, *Fight/Flight,* have the objective of hurting their opponents in some way, getting rid of them, or both. The good of the organization is not a concern at this level. Being right and punishing those who are perceived as wrong predominates. The language used appeals to generalized and personalized principles (such as truth, freedom, and justice) and avoids the specific issue or issues at hand. At this level, the choices have crystallized into two: fighting or fleeing.

Leas described Level V, *Intractable Situations,* as "conflict run amok." Whereas the objective at Level IV is to punish or get the other out of the organization, the objective of individuals in conflict at this fifth level is purely and simply to destroy opponents, irrespective of cost to self or others.

Regarding these five levels, Leas commented: "The first two levels are easy to work with; the third is tough; the fourth and fifth are very difficult and impossible."[2] In other words, conflict at Levels I and II, and sometimes in Level III, can often be handled by normal conflict resolution techniques and can end up being healthy. Much conflict at Level III and most to all of the conflict at Levels IV and V cannot be handled by normal conflict resolution techniques.

Leas added that while it might be the case that the individuals involved in the same conflict are operating on the same level, this is not always true. For example, one person may enter into a conflict with the best of intentions, operating on Level I, *Problems to Solve,* and attempt to use the techniques particularly suited to that level. The other party, however, may be operating at Level IV. In such a situation the first individual, who is attempting to use methods appropriate to Level I, will be suddenly overwhelmed. The situation could be compared to the

---

[2] Speed Leas, "When Conflict Erupts in Your Church: Interview with Speed B. Leas," *Alban Institute Action Information,* vol. 9, no. 5 (1985):16.

differences between dealing with a house cat versus a tiger. In conflict situations it is of paramount importance to recognize the type of individual you are dealing with.

In that regard, superimposing the three types of antagonists (chapter 1) onto Leas's model yields some valuable insights (see Figure 2).

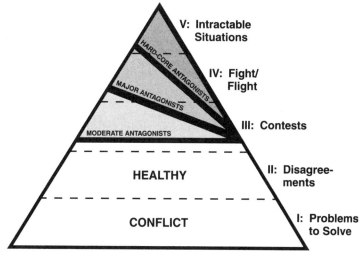

Figure 2: Antagonistic Conflict

As the modified model in Figure 2 shows, the bulk of organizational conflict takes place at healthy, normal levels. The usual methods of conflict resolution are successful in dealing with conflict at the first two levels and, to a limited extent, with conflict at the third. This model also indicates that hard-core antagonists may be found operating at Levels III, IV, and V, major antagonists mainly at Levels III and IV, and moderate antagonists for the most part at Level III.

Healthy resolution of conflict in business and everyday life requires that those involved value one another as human beings,

Part One: Identifying Antagonists

put forth the effort required to understand opposing points of view, and mutually agree that the good of the organization is paramount. Unfortunately, antagonists do none of these consistently. Antagonists are malevolent in intent, falling into that category of people whom M. Scott Peck designates as being evil:

> I have learned nothing in twenty years that would suggest that evil people can be rapidly influenced by any means other than raw power. They do not respond, at least in the short run, to either gentle kindness or any form of spiritual persuasion with which I am familiar.[3]

In antagonistic conflict, the use of techniques appropriate to Level I or Level II conflicts will not work, regardless of how skillfully and creatively they are applied. This book is a resource for dealing specifically with antagonists, who engage in conflict on Levels III, IV, and V.

---

3 M. Scott Peck, *People of the Lie: The Hope for Healing Human Evil* (New York: Simon and Schuster, 1983), p. 68.

CHAPTER **6**

Why Antagonism Happens

WORKPLACES ARE VULNERABLE TO ANTAGONISM, but not uniquely so. Any organization may experience an attack. Loosely defined, an organization is any group of people working together for a common purpose. That purpose might be as widely varied as manufacturing sports equipment, putting out a newspaper, or managing a big-city orchestra. Antagonism occurs in every type of organization and institution: business and industry, profit and nonprofit, universities and schools, retail and manufacturing. You name it, and antagonism can happen there. Why do antagonists exist in so many places? Here are three major factors:

- The nature of antagonists
- The support antagonists receive from others
- The structure of organizations

This chapter will consider each of these factors in turn.

The Nature of Antagonists

Antagonists are antagonistic by nature. If they were not antagonistic in your organization, they would be antagonistic

Part One: Identifying Antagonists

elsewhere. It is their personality. You might wistfully ask, "Why is so-and-so antagonistic?" The simple (if circular) answer is, "Because he or she is an antagonist." It is part of his or her psychological makeup.

Antagonists frequently exhibit *displacement,* the psychological defense mechanism in which the focus of behaviors is shifted to someone other than the individual who first elicited them. The behaviors are displaced because the subject—in this case the antagonist—finds it difficult for various reasons to direct them toward the original object.

The classic example used to illustrate displacement starts with a man being reprimanded by his boss. He comes home and yells at his wife. She in turn shouts at the children. The children kick the dog. The dog chases and bites the cat. The cat claws the living room sofa.

Antagonists displace their angry and hostile behaviors onto people in an organization who too often are easy, available, vulnerable targets. The targets are not the cause of the antagonism, but merely the recipients of it.

Antagonists also exhibit a psychological characteristic called *transference.* The antagonistic individual may unconsciously transfer retained feelings of repressed hostility from childhood to an individual in the present. To an outside and untrained observer, there is no rhyme nor reason for this transfer. Nothing that the recipient of such a transfer of feelings has done would serve to explain it.

Authority can be one trigger of transference. An antagonist may have quite negative feelings toward authority figures in his or her past. The hapless manager or supervisor who then receives the brunt of this hostility would perhaps never begin to suspect that he or she is receiving hostility that "belongs" to another individual from the antagonist's childhood. Obviously, no attempt to change the antagonist's behavior is going to work—deep-seated, unconscious forces are at play in the antagonist.

Support from Others

Antagonists tend to attract followers. The assistance of these followers plays a big part in the escalation of antagonistic conflict. With enough followers an antagonist can take conflicts from teapot tempests to the level of devastating typhoons. Here are some reasons why individuals follow antagonists:

- The truth is often far less exciting than lies and half-truths.
- Bad news is more exciting than good news.
- Some people are gullible, and antagonists take advantage of that.
- Disruptions of lines of authority may create perceived opportunities to "rise in the ranks."
- Antagonists may have personal or informal power that makes people think it is in their best interests to follow them.
- Some people tend to follow orders without question.
- Some people are intimidated by antagonists.
- Some persons just don't want to rock the boat.
- Some people follow antagonists to be one of the crowd.
- Some join antagonists as a way to express their own feelings.

- Some follow antagonists because antagonists frequently make their followers feel important or powerful with special favors, gifts, or compliments.

Followers of antagonists begin to resemble the "moderate antagonists" described in chapter 1, pages 19–20. Most people have a tendency to follow powerful leaders, but those who actively support antagonists have become blind to the actual nature of those they are following.

The Structure of Organizations

Antagonism happens in organizations in part because of the very structure of organizations themselves. Most businesses are relatively small, which makes them ideal places for antagonists to gain the attention they crave. In the United States, for example, approximately 90% of all enterprises are made up of 50 people or fewer. It is an axiom that the smaller an organization is, the more vulnerable it is to attack. And so it is that in the small fishbowl of most organizations, antagonists more easily fill their need for attention—the need to be "big fish." Larger organizations can also be vulnerable at the divisional or departmental level because smaller working entities are usually the places where antagonists get their start.

Business by its very nature also involves competition and struggle—for profits, for market share, for excellence. Conflicts arise within an organization as differing views to accomplish these ends are set forth. The climate of conflict created by competition makes for a broad playing field for antagonists to exercise their destructive ways. For antagonists, it is as though the normal, inevitable conflict of doing business inflames their passion for disruption even more.

At times antagonists have been allowed to operate with near impunity. Managers have either been gun-shy, misguided, or uninformed about how best to deal with them.

The supervisor of a human resources department suggested one reason why antagonists can take hold in an organization. "Our department is responsible for the orientation of new employees," she said. "We sometimes see 'red flags' right away and relay this to the manager responsible for hiring the employee. Most of the time, we are ignored—and most of the time, problems result from that employee."

Sometimes, as a school board member noted, there is also a culture of not dealing with problems. "There was a perception that administrators didn't need to be as 'strong' in an elementary school setting as with middle school or high school. As a result, problems with an obvious antagonist on the faculty were not dealt with in a timely manner. Once he obtained tenure, then it was even more difficult to resolve the situation."

Why does antagonism happen? Because of who antagonists are—their nature. Because some people are ready to follow someone who seems certain of his or her destiny, even when that path leads toward destruction. And because organizational structures themselves often allow antagonism to go unchecked. The opportunity to work in a safe, productive environment, free from antagonism, must be claimed—or reclaimed.

CHAPTER 7

A Question of Values

BEFORE YOU STANDS AN ANTAGONIST—subtle and menacing. Around you are a number of employees, undoubtedly confused, and most certainly with their productivity and effectiveness impaired. What do you do? Doing nothing concedes the antagonist's right to continue behaving destructively, hurting people, reducing team effectiveness, and damaging the organization's mission. Taking decisive action, however, can raise values-charged questions: *How can I legitimately call someone an antagonist? How can I justify my actions to myself—or to others? What is the right thing to do?*

Choices, Choices, Choices

Management choices lie ahead of you. It would be nice if choices were always neatly packaged. Then decisions would be easy. Experience has taught you what reason has always proposed, however: Life is never tidy, seldom easy. Situations sometimes require you to make choices you wish you didn't have to make, even if they are the right choices.

Managers are hired to supervise all the people in their area of responsibility. *All the people* includes the antagonist to be sure, but it should not exclude everyone else. If you have an antagonist among those you are managing, then you have some decisions to make. Who or what will affect your decisions the most? The antagonist? Other employees? Your customers? The mission of your organization? What principles and practices are you going to choose to protect? What and whose values are at stake? Whose rights are at issue, and whose rights should prevail?

Rights and Responsibilities

What rights do antagonists have? They have a right to their opinions and feelings—as long as the exercise of those rights does not take away the rights of anyone else to have their own opinions and feelings. Antagonists have the right of expression— as long as the exercise of that right is not harmful to the organization or to the individuals within that organization and beyond. They have the right to know where they stand. They have a right to feedback about their behavior: how it's coming across to others, how it affects others' perceptions of them, and what the consequences are or will be. Antagonists have a right to their dignity, a right to be respected as human beings. It would be an abuse of their rights for anyone within the organization to deal with them in a disrespectful fashion.

In short, antagonists have the same rights as anybody else in your organization.

It follows, then, that they also have the same responsibilities. Their rights are contained and restricted, just as yours and mine are. No false alarms in crowded theaters. No feeding the information pipeline with lies—because an organization prospers or declines based on its flow of valid information. No one has a right to put a business at risk.

Accept Your Responsibility to Act

The dilemma arises when trying to figure out how to manage an antagonist. Antagonists are not best managed simply by letting them have their way. Common sense asserts that letting antagonists have their way is as unprofessional and as uncaring as letting a small child play with matches or permitting a drunk person to drive a car. Similarly, allowing an antagonist to wreak havoc at the expense of the organization's welfare and the well-being of others is not being a good manager to the antagonist or to others.

Feeding into this decision-making nexus is the risk that the very ones you are trying to help may misunderstand your motives. How will other employees view a manager who assertively confronts a wolf—especially if that wolf happens to be one of them? "Oh, I guess that manager can't stand to have his or her authority challenged." Like it or not, the spotlight is on you, from within and without. What do you do?

Edmund Burke, 18th-century British statesman, strikes a cautionary note here: "The only thing necessary for the triumph of evil is for good men to do nothing." This caution serves to inform the powerful statement attributed to Martin Niemoeller shortly after World War II:

> In Germany they came first for the communists and
> I didn't speak up because I wasn't a communist.
> Then they came for the Jews, and I didn't speak up

because I wasn't a Jew. Then they came for the trade unionists, and I didn't speak up because I wasn't a trade unionist. Then they came for the Catholics, and I didn't speak up because I was a Protestant. Then they came for me, and by that time no one was left to speak up.

The message is clear: You must act.

The Weight of the Matter

Everyone makes judgments all the time, frequently in matters laden with values. Dealing with antagonists is just one of the areas in life where you need to take a close, accurate look and name what you see for what it really is. When you realize you are confronted with an antagonist, you will have to choose how best to deal with that individual. And, like it or not, you *will* deal with the antagonist one way or another.

- You can bury your head in the sand.
- You can take a wait-and-see stance, saying in effect, "If one more person is hurt or leaves, then we'll do something about it."
- You can take definitive action to solve the problem.

Deciding how to deal with antagonists is difficult. Typically there is no perfect solution. Your decision will require some deep soul-searching and reflection, for this is a weighty matter—not one to be entered into lightly.

Realizing that your actions could be painful for the antagonist may cause guilt. "If I can't deal with an antagonist without hurting him or her," you may lament, "then I won't do anything at all." When you realize, however, that doing nothing about the antagonist will result in pain for everyone else, your guilt may be alleviated. "I've seen good, quality employees become exhausted by the turmoil an antagonist creates, throw up their hands, and simply quit," one supervisor related. "Then what happens? The antagonist is in a more powerful position and the beneficiary of having achieved 'seniority' by running off the others."

Rational Decisions, Not Rationalizing

How do you deal with antagonists? What is the caring and fair course to take? Here is a key that may help when you struggle with difficult ethical decisions: Do not let fear guide and direct your response. Fear is a natural and realistic reaction to antagonists. An antagonist can strike back like a rattlesnake. It might seem easier to avoid the problem, but looking the other way results in only a short-term solution. Sometimes, very short. Antagonists will use your inaction against you. Your inability to seize the moment will demonstrate to them that you are not up to the task of leadership as far as they are concerned.

Dealing with antagonists is never easy. No matter what is done, someone will feel pain, be it the antagonist, the organization, or you. But bear in mind that pain is often a necessary precursor to healing. You may never be entirely comfortable with your decision to take action, but difficult and challenging decisions are part of leadership. The very fact that these decisions are difficult for you as a manager indicates that you are a responsible, thoughtful, and considerate leader.

Part Two

Dealing with Antagonists

CHAPTER 8

Coping with Invisible Antagonists

SOMETHING IS HAPPENING. A subtle disturbance within the organization is causing ripples on the surface. The precise source and location of the problem are obscure, but something is stirring. You notice a few signs that little by little add up to trouble. It is as if you were sitting in the woods and suddenly noticed that there were no birds singing and no animal noises to be heard. What now? What can you do?

The situation places you at a disadvantage. You are visible; the antagonist is invisible. One manager in a large organization described the situation like this: "In our organization we called it 'the silent knife'—that deep down worrying feeling about when and where he or she would strike. What an energy stealer this is!" Despite the disadvantages, however, you have a number of options. Some of these may fly in the face of what you would expect or would instinctively do. Here are some positive actions you can take:

1. Be the best possible leader you can be, and continue to do your job effectively. Do everything in your power to

continue to accomplish the goals and objectives of the business or organization you are serving.

2. Don't panic or suspend other activities while you wait for the antagonist to reveal him- or herself. Don't go on a fact-finding mission or expend large amounts of energy searching out the trouble and its source.

3. Continue your general education efforts, as suggested in chapter 19, pages 159–162.

4. If someone mentions rumblings or subterranean stirrings, be direct—"Who is it?" or "I'll be willing to talk with the person"—without coming across as if you need desperately to talk.

5. Accept the fact that it is not critical to precisely identify an antagonist right away. He or she will become evident soon enough. Seeking out the antagonist could cause more trouble than just ignoring the situation for the time being.

6. Act confidently. Remember the operating rule when dealing with antagonists: Weakness invites and prolongs attack; strength repels it. An air of confidence is your best defense.

7. Note the locations of tension and disturbance. If the monthly meetings of a particular group were full of tension in September, October, December, and February, and productive in November and January, check the attendance records. You might find that person X was absent in November and January. Don't exaggerate the importance of the correlation, but pay closer attention to person X. You might have stumbled onto something.

8. A final recourse when you don't know the source of tension is to live with it. People will always be critical, and you will never be in a situation where somebody isn't griping about something. Acknowledge the reality of imperfection in all of life, including the workplace. A problem-free organization is a myth. Recognizing this can help you adapt to this reality.

There is another way in which early tremors can present you with a problem. You personally may be fully aware that a particular individual is an antagonist, but unfortunately you are alone because:

- no one else sees the signs and symptoms; or
- the antagonist may be another leader; or
- others may pretend not to notice (denying the facts); or
- no one else may be willing (thus far) to act.

What can you do when an antagonist is just beginning to make the transition from invisibility to visibility?

For starters, not much—at least not right away. There are two reasons: First, if you lack the support of others, you handicap yourself considerably in dealing effectively with the antagonist. One person who was in a situation where an antagonist was evident to him but to no one else told me: "I could see the self-serving nature of the antagonist very early on, but no one else did. I was left alone, holding this knowledge while my colleagues and others consistently criticized me for making much ado about nothing." Second, sitting back and waiting is sometimes all you can do—and may even be the best possible action. Be patient. By doing so you may allow antagonists the opportunity to publicly reveal themselves. You can also begin to put into place plans for specific education as described in chapter 19 (see page 161).

Invisible antagonists—unseen by you or by others—present you with an opportunity and a challenge. The opportunity is to carry on the mission of the organization. The challenge is to maintain vigilance and be ready to respond, preferably along with others, when an antagonist begins to come forward.

CHAPTER **9**

Handling Indispensable Antagonists

IN A LARGE MEDICAL PRACTICE, the office manager had come to realize that she had an antagonist on her hands—the insurance claims processor. The antagonist's job was complex, demanding, and critical to the smooth operation of the entire office. She dealt with numerous medical insurance companies, each with its own protocols and guidelines. But she was very divisive and constantly provoked and upset others in the office.

The physicians in the practice agreed that the antagonist had received all the warnings she should get and should be terminated. But there was no one ready and able to step in and take over her responsibilities. Nevertheless, after discussing the situation fully with the physicians and their legal counsel, the office manager called the antagonistic insurance claims processor into her office and fired her.

In talking about the situation later, the office manager told me, "It was interesting how the other staff members reacted to the termination. They were angry." She paused briefly, then smiled. "They were angry at me *for not getting rid of her sooner.*"

Part Two: Dealing with Antagonists

The office manager went on to muse about the transitional difficulties the practice experienced. "It was rough for a few weeks. She [the antagonist] had kept some details of her job so close to her vest that we only discovered by trial and error what needed to be done. But the overall stress reduction in the office was well worth the difficulties we experienced while a new person was being trained."

This account sets the stage for pragmatically addressing a thorny problem for businesses and other organizations: What do you do about an antagonist who seems to be indispensable?

Why Antagonists May Seem Indispensable

An antagonist can seem to be indispensable for the same reasons as anyone else. The antagonist may have specialized knowledge or experience. He or she may be directly or indirectly responsible for generating a good deal of revenue, which no company would lightly give up. Or the antagonist may have important contacts up, down, or sideways that make him or her valuable.

Here are some examples:

- *Knowledge.* "Sharon has personally put together our entire data processing system. No one else understands it, and its structure is not written down anywhere. We'd be out of business in three weeks if the system went down. Sharon is indispensable."
- *Revenue generation.* "I'd deal with Bill's undermining and attacks in a minute, but he has consistently run up the best record in sales month after month. Our whole department's

record would look bad, and the company would suffer significant income loss if Bill left. Bill is indispensable."

- *Outside contacts.* "Juanita is the only one who has strong contacts with the city zoning officer and with the mayor's office. Without Juanita, our expansion plans might take twice as long to get approval, and we'd be lucky to move half as fast as we do now. Juanita is indispensable."
- *Downside contacts.* "Malcolm has so ingratiated himself with the people in the print shop and many on the plant floor that I wonder how many would leave if Malcolm did. He's said more than once, 'If I leave, a number of other people will go, too.' We can't afford a mass exodus. Malcolm is indispensable."
- *Upside contacts.* "I'd get rid of Joe if it weren't for the fact that he plays golf with one of the vice presidents. If push came to shove, I'm sure I'd just be told to back off. Joe is indispensable."

In the minds of their supervisors, each one of these antagonists is invulnerable to firm steps and discipline because of the personal costs, organizational costs, or both. Each one is presumed to be indispensable. These managers are apparently caught between a rock and a hard place, in a lose/lose situation.

Weighing the Diagnosis of Antagonism

One vital question to pose before continuing: Are you sure the person in question is an antagonist? Or is this person just a maverick? Mavericks can be difficult to manage and might not be worth the effort if it weren't for one fact: They produce. They may break rules, ignore the home office, fail to keep up with paperwork—and they produce. As long as mavericks fit within your organizational system and their behavior does not negatively affect the morale of those who work with them, a smart manager may choose to create a situation in which they can work well and be extremely productive.

Good diagnosis is important, therefore. A maverick is someone who may indeed rock the boat; an antagonist could sink it. Is the person attacking *the job* with passion (albeit sometimes without proper regard for procedure), or is the person attacking *other people?* The one who is determined to complete a project is probably a maverick; the one attacking people is probably an antagonist.

You can get caught up in the heat of the moment and forget that there are clear and unmistakable signs that you are dealing with an antagonist. Part one of this book, "Identifying Antagonists," gives a clear picture of the signs of a true antagonist. Refer back to chapters 1–3, the diagnostic chapters. Reflect on the definition of antagonism in chapter 1. Review the personality characteristics in chapter 2. Match the red flags signifying an antagonist—in chapter 3—to the person you are dealing with. When the behaviors signaled by those diagnostic markers multiply, it is time to do something about the situation.

Weighing Professional and Personal Issues

As you weigh the apparent loss to the organization, there are several professional and personal issues to consider. Questions that you need to examine and answer are ones such as these:

- *What is your responsibility to your department or organization?* Answers to this question have already been suggested in chapter 7 on values. If you believe in the mission of the organization, then the organization is certainly worthy of your unwavering protection.

- *What is your responsibility to the employees of your department or organization, those who may be in the line of fire?* When an antagonist is rampaging, people get hurt, their security is placed in jeopardy, their productivity and morale suffer, and they are distracted by rumors and gossip. These employees are worthy of your protection.

- *What does work mean to you?* Work is undoubtedly a significant part of your life. Beyond providing a livelihood, satisfaction on the job can go far to give meaning and purpose to your life. Antagonistic attacks tear at this satisfaction, interfere with your productivity, and can harm your promotability and potential for increased earnings. Your work and your morale are worthy of your protection.

- *What does quality of life mean to you?* If an antagonist is lurching about in the china shop confines of your life, a lot of fragile items are at risk. Your health is one of them. How well are you sleeping at night, caught up in the carnage of an antagonistic attack? How much heartburn medication are you taking, or have matters progressed beyond the heartburn stage? Is your blood pressure affected? Then there's depression, weight gain, alcohol consumption, being accident-prone because of inattentiveness, and the like. Self-protection is a basic need. Emotional availability to those you love also counts here. If you are shouldering the burdens of Atlas when you come home from work, your loved ones are not getting what they need from you, nor are you able to appreciate what they have to offer you.

Your health, your morale, and your family are worthy of protection.

Antagonists threaten your organization's welfare and the well-being of other employees. They threaten your own work life, your vocation, your personal life or health, and perhaps even the quality of life of those you love. All these threats call for protective measures.

Weighing the Assumptions of Indispensability

In the light of these professional and personal considerations, you may need to re-examine the assumptions of indispensability. Often, "indispensable" antagonists only appear to be indispensable, but this perception may put blinders on managers. These blinders may interfere with first recognizing the problem and then with taking firm and responsible action. Trusting that the department or organization will not only survive but thrive without the presumed indispensable individual may be a startling thought. Yet even in the short term, when an antagonist is dealt with definitively, the gains for you, the organization, and other employees can be almost immediate.

What will happen to us tomorrow if _____ is no longer working for us? That's the question that commonly plagues managers when they consider the fallout from taking action with an antagonist. Better questions, however, are: Where will we be in a year if we don't take action? What might our workplace be like if we do take action?

Yes, there will be loss. Whatever factors go into making the antagonist seem indispensable—the person's knowledge, revenue-generation, contacts, and the like—will be gone. One of the worries you may have to deal with, for example, is whether other employees will leave when you take firm action with the antagonist. If others leave, it may be unfortunate, but not as bad as leaving the antagonist free to run riot. Consider the possibility that there may be some unexpected benefits when others leave as well.

It is important that you and other leaders act toward the antagonist as if he or she were not indispensable—and be prepared to back up your convictions with actions. The time may come when you need to make a surgical decision: This gangrenous limb must come off, or the whole organism will die.

A Plan of Action

When it becomes obvious that an apparently indispensable antagonist must be dealt with, here are some concrete steps you can take.

- *Whatever you do, do it sooner rather than later.* Nothing is so bad now that more time will not simply make it worse. "Doing it sooner" will have fewer side effects and consequences than doing it later.

- *Practice damage control and problem avoidance.* With the plethora of laws protecting employees from discrimination in the workplace, discipline and discharge decisions can be veritable minefields. Always consult with your human resources professionals and counsel, as appropriate, when you are contemplating termination or discipline to deal with an antagonist. Prior planning and consultation will help avoid creating any further leverage for the antagonist to bring discrimination or wrongful discharge claims against the organization.

- *Communicate with other leaders.* As a simple matter of courtesy and good practice, inform your superiors and peers of your plan for dealing with the antagonist, whether that plan is limit-setting, disciplinary action, termination, or whatever. They need to know enough history to understand your rationale. Communicating the reasons for discipline or discharge must be held in confidence, however. While it is legal to communicate about the situation and the reasons for action to a select group, spreading such information beyond the discrete "need to know" group is an invitation to a libel or slander lawsuit.

- *Enlist support, as needed.* If your organization has done general education about antagonism, (see chapter 19, pages 159–160), you may need to remind other leaders of the principles discussed in that chapter to help them understand what is going on and why you are employing the actions you have decided to take. In addition, you and other leaders may need to use the phalanx technique (see chapter 12, pages 101–104) in order to deal successfully with the antagonist together.

- *Inform others, as much as is appropriate, inside and outside the organization.* Sometimes customers, vendors, or other employees need to know what is happening. There are confidentiality matters to take into account, however, as well as matters of decorum and "not airing your dirty laundry." But within those boundaries there is still wide latitude for you to communicate crisply and clearly what is going on, whether in writing or verbally. Here's an example of a brief, to-the-point memo that says enough to other employees:

> As of today, _____ has left XYZ Company. All questions or issues related to covering _____'s work responsibilities should be directed to _____. Please refer any questions you may have about the change to your supervisor.

Get legal advice if you have any questions whatsoever about the appropriateness of any communication you are considering or comments you may wish to make.

- *Once you have made a decision, don't look over your shoulder for approval after the fact.* Go ahead and do what you need to do, and save the organization the pain of constantly second-guessing the decision. There is a temptation to seek affirmation again and again: "That was all right, wasn't it?" If you have the consensual validation of those from whom it matters, don't worry about getting it from everyone.

- *If others leave because the antagonist leaves, accept it as a necessary cost.* In some cases it may not be a cost at all but a benefit that those others left, especially if they were in sympathy with the antagonist. It is unfortunate if some innocently duped persons leave, but aside from communicating clearly what was going on within the bounds of decorum and legality, you can't control what they may choose to do.

- *Mobilize alternatives to getting the organization's work done.* Be ready to step in with resources to make the best transition you can after you have dealt with the antagonist. Bring in other staff who have been cross-trained.

Temporary services might supply some of the help you need. Perhaps you could bring someone out of retirement for a while who can hold up the end of the business for which the antagonist had been responsible. Realize that you may have alternatives. If you have to delay some projects or scale back temporarily, the cost may be bearable and better than the high cost of maintaining the antagonist.

The bottom line in dealing with antagonists is that there is really no such thing as an indispensable person. The peace of mind you can reach immediately will make even the short-term effects more of a benefit than a loss. No matter what the short-term effects, the long-term good of the organization and its employees will certainly be best served by dealing with the antagonist effectively and in a timely fashion.

CHAPTER 10

Dealing with Antagonists in Group Settings

Any meeting or group situation with an active antagonist present has the potential to degenerate into a three-ring circus featuring the antagonist as ringmaster. Consciously or unconsciously, antagonists carry two questions into group situations: How can I disrupt? How can I get control? Whether a group will tend toward chaos or maintain orderly flow and continue to accomplish the business at hand depends on how you and the rest of the group respond.

Note the phrase *you and the rest of the group*. The group collectively has a force greater than the sum of its parts. This underscores the importance of general education (see chapter 19) about antagonism before an antagonist ever emerges. When others understand that containing an antagonist is the joint responsibility of the entire group, this will increase the chances of accomplishing what needs to be done and muting the effect of an antagonist.

Part Two: Dealing with Antagonists

How Antagonists Act in Group Situations

Here are some behaviors that antagonists may display in group situations. Note that nonantagonists simply do not behave this way.

- *"Me and three others."* When offering criticism, antagonists refer not only to themselves but also frequently to others who supposedly feel the same way. Sometimes antagonists even pretend that they themselves do not have criticisms; they are just carrying a message for those not willing or "too afraid" to speak up on their own. Criticism itself is not the issue. Nonantagonists do offer criticism, sometimes even strong criticism, but only antagonists will talk right away about anonymous others—and refuse to give further details or name names.

- *Obvious disinterest.* Antagonists sometimes show their disdain in a group setting by acting totally bored, as if the information is stupid or pointless. Thumbing through a calendar or palm pilot, working on another project during the meeting, reading mail or e-mail can all be used to indicate how unimportant the antagonist considers the meeting. One manager noted that the antagonist he was dealing with often evidenced "dramatic inattention" by sighing loudly during presentations. At the other extreme, a nursing coordinator told me that an antagonist was able to manipulate a meeting by being so unusually quiet that others began asking what was wrong. Then the antagonist had the perfect opening to pontificate on her views.

- *Sniping.* The antagonist continually takes potshots at others, especially leaders. Hardly a meeting goes by, for example, without the antagonist finding fault with something or making snide insinuations about his or her chosen victim.

- *"Look at me!"* Antagonists often use constant movement to disrupt a meeting or to focus attention on themselves. "I just can't stand crooked pictures," was one antagonist's apology for getting up at an important point in a meeting and straightening a picture on the wall. A village board chairman related another tale of an antagonist's disruptive behavior at a meeting: "Although Joe was the second person to the meeting room, he went to the refreshment table to get a glass of water after the meeting had already started. The second trip was for a cup of coffee. After finishing the coffee, he tapped his pencil on the cup several times before getting up for more coffee and a doughnut. Each time he got up, he managed to draw everyone's attention away from the business at hand."

- *"I beg to differ."* Antagonists disagree with you and others monotonously, trivially, and predictably. Their having a different opinion is not the issue. It's their making a big issue about differing with you.

- *According to the book.* If a meeting is formal and using *Robert's Rules of Order* or similar guidelines, an antagonist may exploit these parliamentary procedures to embarrass those in charge, to manipulate the group, or to stymie the results of any discussion.

- *Smirking and grimacing.* Antagonists may make faces to others or roll their eyes while a leader is speaking, many times in such a way that the leader will see them. After a leader makes a point, the antagonist may also make a comment to an individual seated close by, sometimes accompanied by a laugh or smile.

- *Backseat driving.* Another method antagonists can use to disrupt meetings or make new leaders look inept is by "helping" them run a meeting. A new supervisor told me how an antagonist, in the sweetest, most patient tones, constantly corrected him in front of the group or made suggestions about the way the meeting should be conducted. "Don't you want to . . ." or "Wouldn't it be better if we . . ." she would say, relishing the supervisor's obvious discomfort.

- *Crowd poaching.* Occasionally something over which a speaker or presenter has little or no control will go wrong—the audio system misbehaves, a visual display is out of sync, or the presenter trips on the way to the podium. Crowds usually get antsy, signaled by shifting and fidgeting, looking away from the platform, and the like. An antagonist may seize this opportunity to diminish the speaker even further than circumstances have already done. The leader's vulnerability is a signal to the antagonist to try and poach control of the crowd by cracking a joke at the leader's expense, for example, or making a comment in a loud stage whisper. Antagonists are quick to smell any weakness and use it as a chance to discredit someone.

- *Verbal domination.* Probably the most blatant maneuver an antagonist can make is to try to take verbal control of the meeting. Sarcasm, browbeating, insulting, belaboring points, dragging up past issues or history, or attempting outright to change the subject are all tools in an antagonist's arsenal. "They simply wear out everyone with arguments," one team leader told me.

How to Handle Antagonists in Group Situations

When you see these or other evidences of an antagonist creating disturbances in a group, here are some ways to handle the situation.

1. Let the group take care of the situation, if at all possible. Intervention is much more powerful coming from a group member than from a leader. If you are the group leader, step in only if the antagonist is getting out of hand.
2. Simply state a noncommittal "Thanks for your input," and then move right on to the next item on the agenda.
3. Sometimes you might want to listen well to an antagonist, but don't deny or agree with his or her comments. Given enough rope, an antagonist sometimes hangs him- or herself.
4. Interrupt in a calm, powerful manner any antagonistic tirade that seems to be going nowhere: "We have an important agenda to get done. If you have a specific recommendation, let's hear it. Otherwise, I propose we move on."
5. If time has been set on the agenda for an antagonist who wants to raise an issue, limit the time he or she is allowed

to speak. Tell the antagonist in advance his or her time allotment (the shorter the better), and stick to this decision.

6. If the antagonist goes over the designated time, break in and remind the individual that the time allowance had been previously established. Even if the antagonist hasn't finished, excuse him or her. As one leader noted, the most overt ploy of an antagonist is to monopolize time, "almost like a filibuster in Congress, chewing up time to prevent work on the task at hand."

7. If the antagonist insists on returning to the same disruptive topic, tell him or her: "We have heard you out; the issue has been dealt with and resolved. We have nothing further to discuss." If the antagonist insists sometime later to have "new evidence," you can once again remind the individual that the issue has been resolved and will not be discussed again.

Antagonists in group situations respond to specific applications of the principles of strength and assertiveness. Keep a level head and be matter-of-fact about the necessity of getting on with the business of the group. You can count on the certainty that most members of the group want to do just that.

CHAPTER **11**

Mobilizing the Management Team

When an antagonist is creating his or her special brand of havoc, who is responsible for dealing with the antagonist and the problems he or she causes? Everyone. Whether a CEO, a line manager, or other employee—all are responsible collectively.

An organization is uniquely structured to undertake this obligation because it exists as a body. This is more than an accident of word choice, more than even a legal nicety. Antagonism is like a virulent disease in that body, posing a threat not just to an isolated organ (the original person or persons attacked), but to the entire organism. The entire organism suffers until the disease is overcome, and the whole body must work to overcome it. A Zulu saying illustrates this concept well: "When there is a thorn in the big toe, the whole body stoops to pluck it out."

Antagonists are very adept at employing divide-and-conquer tactics. An attitude that "we're all in this together" provides an immensely powerful, effective antidote to the disruptive poisons of antagonism.

Communicate with Other Leaders

Leaders frequently complain that they are the last to know there is trouble of any kind. Leaders—your supervisor and other managers who could be affected—should be kept informed of potentially antagonistic situations for a number of reasons.

- They can be much more effective if not caught unawares by the situation.
- They may be able to provide some crucial advice, insights, or assistance at an earlier stage.
- They might be in a position to arrange for extra help in dealing with the situation.

Leaders want to know when a storm is beginning to brew, not when all they can do is help clean up the wreckage.

Antagonists might also make threats such as, "I'm going to call (name)." You can experience peace of mind, knowing the appropriate manager already knows about the situation, and unperturbedly reply, "(Name) is already aware of this." Offer no further explanation.

It is also important for other leaders to know the history of the problem. Is it new or of long standing? Has this individual behaved like this before? They also need to know if the situation involves just one person or more than one. Other leaders will want to know who else knows about the situation, whether it's other members of the management team or other staff.

Communicate Objectively

In communicating with others, be objective. Report facts. Avoid subjective statements or generalizations about the antagonist. Concentrate on describing behaviors. Be prepared to give actual examples, with as many facts as possible to substantiate your observations. The following example clarifies the distinction between subjective and objective reporting.

Subjective	**Objective**
John was extremely disruptive, combative, and threatening at the meeting yesterday! He attacked me and my leadership, totally inappropriately, undermining my authority in the eyes of everyone at the meeting.	At the meeting, John stood up and started talking without being recognized by the leader, whom he accused of "selling out to the competition." When asked what his specific objections were to the plan, John kept repeating rather loudly, "I know what you are up to. You can't fool me." After asking for John's specific objections a number of times, the leader politely asked him to sit down. As he did so, John said, "Just wait until the boss hears about this!"

Subjective reports are too limited. In the subjective report, the reader merely found out that the writer has rather strong emotions about the subject and thinks John behaved poorly. In the objective report, the official received facts: the who, what, when, where, and how. If a manager or supervisor reads that so-and-so was pugnacious and out of control, inevitably he or

Part Two: Dealing with Antagonists

she will think, *That's just an opinion.* But by letting the facts do the talking, the writer of the objective description lets the reader form his or her own opinions.

At all levels, employees must be confident that leaders will not allow themselves to be manipulated, by circumstances or by the antagonist, into decisions that may have a short-term gain but result in a long-term loss. Whether you are a CEO, manager, or other supervisor, you are the one who holds the life of your organization—its short-term good and long-term well-being—in your hands.

CHAPTER **12**

Four Specific Leadership Strategies

THIS BOOK HAS LEADERSHIP AS ITS ENTIRE SUBJECT, leadership in the very specific area of defending one's workplace, its mission, and one's staff from harm by antagonists. Leaders, for the most part, are confronted with the hard, practical necessities of responding and taking action. Four focused leadership strategies are covered in this chapter.

The Phalanx: A Unified Front

A phalanx is a military tactic developed by the ancient Greeks that involved a well-armed infantry unit standing shoulder-to-shoulder, shield-to-shield, about eight men deep, forming a mobile, almost impenetrable wall of defense.

The lesson for organizations that face the attacks of antagonists is that all staff, leaders in particular, would do well to form a phalanx when dealing with antagonists. Organizational shields are not composed of bronze and leather, but of the spirit of working together, seeing with the same set of eyes, united against the attacker. The success of your phalanx depends greatly on the degree to which leaders function as a consistent, unified whole.

Part Two: Dealing with Antagonists

An important preliminary step forward in developing an impenetrable phalanx is an extensive educational process as discussed in chapter 19. Include as many of the staff as appropriate—especially those in the direct line of fire as well as those who can directly help.

Adopt the phalanx tactic when roads to reconciliation have failed but before serious damage is done by an antagonist. John Wooden talks about the importance of doing your team building before the big game: "I liked to think that by game time my work was virtually done, that I could almost go up into the stands and watch the game without saying a word because my team was so well prepared."[1]

The goal of the phalanx is the extinction of divisive actions within your organization or department. *Extinction* is the process by which certain behaviors are eliminated through nonreinforcement. With antagonists, this means refraining from favoring them with further attention, which only serves to reinforce their destructive behavior. For example, don't set up a special group to try to deal with the antagonist through a lengthy series of meetings. This only gives the antagonist the attention he or she craves—and exhausts good people. If the leadership and other employees stop reinforcing the antagonist's divisive actions, he or she will lose power rapidly.

Establish an informal hotline, so that when an antagonist contacts one leader, information can be quickly shared with other leaders who need to know. This communication pipleline has two purposes:

---

[1] Wooden, John with Steve Jamison, *Wooden: A Lifetime of Observations and Reflections On and Off the Court* (Chicago: Contemporary Books, 1997), p.159.

1. The group can immediately support the first person that the antagonist contacts.
2. When the antagonist approaches the next person in the group, that individual already knows what the antagonist has said to the first person.

The decision to extinguish antagonistic behavior takes place after your organizational leadership has determined that attempts at reconciliation have failed and that lending a sympathetic ear to the antagonist is no longer appropriate. Make no mistake, extinguishing antagonistic behavior requires a great deal of conscious effort by all. Much progress toward nonreinforcement can be sabotaged by a single leader deciding to operate independently, thinking it won't hurt to lend a sympathetic ear to the antagonist "just once." In truth it will hurt, because any kind of reinforcement will induce the antagonist to continue or escalate his or her destructive behavior. Strive for a defense that is rock solid and leakproof—a shutdown of the attention and reactions that keep an antagonist fueled up and active. Establishing and maintaining a phalanx means each leader agrees that no one operates independently when confronted by the antagonist.

In an organization I consulted with, an antagonist sent separate harshly indicting letters to several members of the upper-level management team. The team's response was for everyone to bring the letters they received to a meeting and share them with one another. This ruined the effect. A hapless follower of the antagonist who asked about the letters was told nonchalantly by one of the leaders, "Oh, yes—we all brought our letters in and shared them with each other." This message clearly says, *and we are not divided*. The chief aim of that antagonist—

divisiveness—failed because of the excellent communication of that management team.

Enlist Support from Relevant Staff

Those in leadership positions will also function better if as many as possible in the workplace take responsibility for dealing with antagonists. If you are a leader, it would be wise for you to educate as many as appropriate to empower them to work in this area right alongside you. This should be on a need-to-know basis, however.

By building a supportive community among those who work closely with you, you will be personally supported and empowered to deal with antagonists in a way that will make a significant difference. Your staff, who might be confused to see you operating outside of your usual style in your dealings with an antagonist, need to be brought into the picture as much as it is reasonable and legal to do so. An antagonist is intent on giving you a world of grief; an informed and knowledgeable staff can shield you to some extent, by screening incoming calls, for example, and referring an antagonist to the individual within the organization who should properly handle his or her request.

Your staff's supportive attitude is at least as important as their supportive actions. Ideally you hope your staff will perceive the reality of the antagonist's attack with the same clarity you do. General education is always appropriate at every level, and specific education may be necessary for some who work with you. You need their support. And this support will not be just one-way. You will offer as much support as you receive, because that spirit of working together, when it prevails, is one of the most effective ways to blunt an antagonist's attack.

Disciplinary Measures

By the time matters have reached the stage where a phalanx is called for, it may be that disciplinary measures appropriate to your own setting are also needed. Organizations vary in their respective approaches to discipline, and there is sometimes a reluctance on the part of leaders and managers to apply needed discipline. The result is that, while disciplinary procedures exist on the books, organizations sometimes make every effort to avoid putting them into practice.

In the case of antagonists, this reluctance is extremely unfortunate and inappropriate. There is no room for improvisation. Placating antagonists is useless, even counterproductive, and often promotes further disruption and divisiveness. In the movie *Thirteen Days,* about President John F. Kennedy's handling of the Cuban missile crisis in 1962, one of the characters uttered a statement about the situation: "Appeasement only makes the aggressor more aggressive." This is true, as well, when dealing with an antagonist. Appeasement only makes an antagonist more antagonistic.

Since it is obvious that antagonists have problems, you might imagine recommending professional counseling or psychotherapy for them out of concern for their personal well-being and your desire to prevent full-blown antagonism. Although the idea of recommending counseling sounds worthwhile on the surface, it is generally futile and could be legally dangerous.

First of all, because of their personality makeup, antagonists very rarely follow through on a recommendation of counseling. If they view everyone else as wrong and themselves as right, why should they seek help? In addition, antagonists may perceive your recommendation of professional help as a personal threat, significantly increasing the likelihood that they will lash out at you.

Very importantly, recommending that someone get medical or psychological treatment can call into play the Americans with Disabilities Act (ADA). Suggesting such treatment can lead to a deduction by a jury or counsel that an individual was "regarded as" disabled and discriminated against because of the perception of disability. This could create a cause of action under the ADA.

Some companies have an Employee Assistance Program (EAP) or an equivalent for dealing with problem employees. As a start, you could recommend the antagonist be sent to your EAP for interpersonal skills or sensitivity training. If your company does have some form of EAP or other formal procedures, follow them meticulously.

If you think the antagonist is breaking the law, consult a lawyer or the proper authorities. If the antagonist breaks the law, leaders owe it to the organization and its employees to have the wrong reported. This can also serve to clarify the thinking of those who may be uncertain as to whether the antagonist's actions are injurious or destructive.

The judicious and consistent use of the disciplinary measures available to you by company policy or procedures is vital in dealing with the destructive behavior of antagonists.

Use Your Authority

The definition of antagonists has already specified that they tend to single out leaders for their special brand of havoc. How you and other leaders in your organization respond, therefore, is crucial. People may not always like strong leaders, but they despise weak ones. To earn the respect of those you lead, use your authority, but use it wisely.

The limits of your authority will vary from position to position and from organization to organization. Know the extent of your authority with regard to your organization and your job description. When you do need to use your authority, use it very effectively and with a great deal of strength.

Failure to use the authority of your position represents more than just your private decision. In most organizations, you derive the power of your position from the act of superiors who have placed you in that position and entrusted you with the well-being and productivity of those you supervise. Therefore, if you do not act with proper authority when antagonism interferes with the mission and objectives of your workplace, it actually becomes the organization's refusal to respond to the situation.

When managing people is part of your job description and your identity, it can certainly be frustrating to realize that you can do little or nothing to help antagonists change. Good management is not sufficient to handle an antagonist. The hardened will of an antagonist can perhaps only be changed by experiencing the consequences of his or her behavior. You, as a leader, are entrusted with plenty of responsibilities, including concern for the antagonist. But your primary function is to care for and protect the organizational mission for which you are responsible.

CHAPTER **13**

How to Handle a One-to-One Meeting with an Antagonist

TENSION. IT FILLS THE ROOM, pressing in on you and making it hard for you to breathe. You want to focus on the individual seated across from you, but when your eyes meet, you are the first to look away. You can feel the other person looking at you with a pitiless, hostile stare, icy and implacable.

Your mind flits uncertainly from one question to the next: *What do I say? What can I do? How should I act? Will reason work? Maybe if I could show that I care.* Round and round you go.

The other person, who is expressing "concerns" about you and your leadership, seems oblivious to the tension, a study in composure and self-confidence. It is only too clear who wrote the script, assigned you the tragic part, and now directs the production: the antagonist.

Does a meeting with an antagonist have to be like this? Absolutely not!

Who should guide the interaction? is the key question in dealing with antagonists. The antagonist's goal is to control you

Part Two: Dealing with Antagonists

and the situation. If the antagonist is able to gain that control, the potential harm to you and your department or organization is incalculable. Your goal when meeting with an antagonist is to take charge of *yourself.* When you manage yourself and certain environmental factors well in such a meeting, you will manage the situation much better—and you will also handle the antagonist much better.

You will approach a meeting with an antagonist much differently than with other people. The recommendations and concepts in this chapter are not suitable to use with individuals who are not antagonists because you simply would not relate to most people this way. But antagonists are not "most people" and warrant a much firmer approach.

You may be tempted to reject the principles in this chapter because they are so counterintuitive to what you know about quality relating. But keep this key in mind: The purpose of any interaction or conversation with an antagonist is to demonstrate calm confidence and strength, not to try to reason with or convince him or her of anything. The characteristics of antagonists demand firm, assertive behavior when you interact with them. To act otherwise is to court failure.

It should be noted that, as a leader, you may need to talk with an antagonist about ongoing work-related issues. These kinds of interactions are not the subject of this chapter. You would be wise in these situations, however, to proceed as if you were handling porcupines. The type of meeting discussed in this chapter is one intiated by an antagonist to "share concerns."

To prevent a meeting intiated by an antagonist from becoming the kind of disaster noted at the beginning of this chapter, consider three components of a meeting that you need to manage:

- Setting up the meeting
- The arrival of the antagonist
- The meeting itself

The principles and practices that follow demonstrate strength, and any demonstration of strength when dealing with antagonists lessens their effectiveness.

Setting Up the Meeting

Setting up the meeting begins at the point an antagonist contacts you and ends when he or she arrives to talk. These preliminaries may appear to be insignificant, but they are crucial for setting a tone for everything that follows.

Who Contacts Whom?

You might be tempted to think that initiating a meeting will be the best way to clear up misunderstandings. Resist that temptation. Meeting with an antagonist might temporarily quiet him or her, but not for long. You will end up sacrificing self-respect, self-control, and control of the situation. If antagonists are able to entice you to reach out to them, you demonstrate weakness and vulnerability in their eyes—and they will capitalize on it. Antagonists do not respond positively to attempts at conciliation.

If there is to be a meeting, it should be at the antagonist's initiative. Of all the variables discussed in this chapter, this one is the most important. If you make the initial contact, you communicate to the antagonist that you are the one really needing to get together and talk. You would be placing the antagonist in control from the beginning.

The presumption—that the antagonist is initiating the meeting, not you—is very important to all that follows. You are not planning to discuss the antagonist's work performance. You are not planning to inform the antagonist of pending disciplinary actions. You are not planning to "resolve the differences" between you. You are agreeing to a meeting the antagonist wants to have so that the antagonist may "share concerns" or offer whatever else may be on his or her mind.

The exception to this principle of your not initiating a meeting with an antagonist is when you are in the process of taking firm action (see chapter 12). When you are ready once and for all to deal with the problem, after consulting legal counsel, only then should you—together with other leaders—initiate a meeting with an antagonist.

Where Do You Meet?

The location of a meeting with an antagonist is a critical factor. Antagonists sometimes suggest that you meet in their office or work area. Meeting with them on their turf only gives them added confidence. Avoid this by suggesting an alternative, "Let's meet in my office. We'll be able to talk there just fine."

Be firm in your intention to meet in a place of your choosing. If you do not have an office or similar convenient place in which to meet, you may even want to use someone else's. You could also arrange to meet in a conference or other meeting room. A neutral location is preferable to a place of the

How to Handle a One-to-One Meeting with an Antagonist

antagonist's choosing. Stick to the principle: You choose the meeting place.

"How about Lunch?"

Antagonists will occasionally invite you to have lunch with them in order to discuss their vexations. You are better off not accepting that arrangement. A meal creates an unwanted atmosphere of intimacy that will work against you. You may be the intended main course!

If you meet with an antagonist for lunch, you face a number of problems. There would undoubtedly be interruptions, and you would not be free to use many of the tactics discussed in this chapter to maintain control of yourself and of the situation. Certain actions demonstrating firmness can be done in an office that would be inappropriate in public. There is also the question of who pays for lunch. Antagonists like to pick up the tab, thereby asserting a measure of control over you.

If an antagonistic individual says that he or she wants to meet about serious concerns and suggests a lunch engagement, calmly say something like, "I think it would be better if we met in my office." If the antagonist persists, continue to assert your own wishes. Don't allow yourself to be taken to lunch. The time for you to establish control is when you set up the meeting, not at a busy eating establishment.

"Can I Come Over Right Now?"

Sometimes an antagonist will call or stop by your office with an air of urgency and ask (or demand) to meet with you right away. What do you do? First of all, ask the antagonist what he or she needs to talk to you about. The person might be involved in a work-related issue and be in genuine need of help. If so, by all means meet with the antagonist as you would with any other employee who needs direction. If the individual tells you that the issue is with your leadership or related subjects, however, that is different. Permitting the antagonist to intrude on your schedule amounts to handing over control of the situation. Don't do it. If the antagonist refuses to tell you what he or she wants to discuss, it probably does not need immediate attention. You might want to say something like, "This is not a good time right now. What about getting together tomorrow morning at 11:30 for a half hour?" You need not be more specific than that. Your schedule is your own business. Should the antagonist demand to know specifically why you can't meet right away, you can simply say, "It's not possible right now."

When Do You Meet?

Along with not meeting immediately at an antagonist's request, it is inadvisable to meet at any specific time the antagonist suggests, even when this might be possible for you. It is, again, a matter of taking charge of the situation: You determine the time. If an antagonist suggests that you meet at 9:00 A.M. the next day, you may want to say something like, "Nine is not a good time for me. How about 11:30? We can sit down for half an hour at that time."

Since antagonists tend to think they have the right to take liberties with your schedule, this approach permits you to control the timing of the meeting, not only when it will take place but for how long. Most of the time antagonists will not take issue with your setting a time limit. If they demand more time, you could respond by saying, "I think we ought to be

How to Handle a One-to-One Meeting with an Antagonist

able to deal with everything in thirty minutes if we are efficient about it." Don't be forced into setting up an open-ended meeting or setting aside more time than you wish to give. By doing so, you start out on the wrong foot, giving the antagonist control of that aspect of the situation, which is contrary to your best interests. Furthermore, the dogged persistence of antagonists tends to wear people down. Meeting with an antagonist at length weakens your resistance, aiding and abetting the antagonist's cause.

If possible, schedule your meeting with an antagonist before another commitment. If you arrange your schedule this way, be sure to end your meeting with the antagonist promptly when the time is up. Don't fall into the trap of extending the meeting. This not only is disrespectful to your other commitments, but it also gives the antagonist a degree of power over you. Gently but firmly cutting off antagonists at the scheduled ending time demonstrates your authority. Even though it may temporarily upset them, it will prove beneficial in the long run.

The Arrival of the Antagonist

This section covers the time period between the antagonist's arrival for the meeting and when the substantive portion of the meeting begins. What happens during this arrival period is crucial. Some of these recommendations may be applied more easily if you have an office of your own. If you don't, apply as many of the principles as you can.

When Do You Begin?

Whether you begin early, on time, or somewhat late can subtly influence the tone of the meeting and determine who will be

Part Two: Dealing with Antagonists

in charge of the situation. It is inadvisable to begin early because this conveys to the antagonist your willingness to be accommodating, which the antagonist will be quick to interpret as a sign of weakness. The fact that you see yourself as a representative of reasonableness and decency must not blind you to the nature of the person you are dealing with: Antagonists are on the prowl for signs of weakness, which they will then attempt to exploit.

Some antagonists make a practice of arriving early. Not anticipating this can catch you off guard and put you at a distinct disadvantage. If you have an administrative assistant, advise him or her ahead of time to invite the antagonist to have a seat. If you don't have an assistant, anticipate the antagonist's possible early arrival by having your door shut. If the antagonist arrives early and knocks on your door, open it slightly and say, "I'll be out in a few minutes." If you don't have a private office, plan on arriving at the designated meeting location precisely at the agreed-upon time for the meeting.

Other antagonists arrive late to try to establish control in their favor. If the antagonist who has requested a meeting with you is late, engage in some other task in the interim, such as returning a telephone call, but don't cut your conversation short when the antagonist arrives. Completing your call treats the other individual with respect and communicates to the antagonist that your time is valuable and you will not waste it.

If the antagonist asks about the delay, calmly reply that you were ready at the scheduled time, but since he or she was not there, you returned a telephone call. That's the truth, and the truth is difficult to dispute. Don't let the antagonist use his or

How to Handle a One-to-One Meeting with an Antagonist

her tardiness, however, as an excuse to extend the meeting beyond the time frame that you had originally established.

How Do You Greet the Antagonist?

Perhaps you typically greet people with a friendly smile and a cheery hello, paving the way for them to share their needs and concerns with you. With an antagonist, however, your greeting might well be different. Ask yourself if you are in fact genuinely happy to see him or her. Respond to an antagonist in a way that is more congruent with how you feel. A simple hello spoken in a businesslike tone would suffice. An ambiguous greeting, disclosing little about your feelings, prevents an antagonist from being deluded into thinking that he or she has control of you and of the conversation.

What about Seating?

Who sits first? This might seem unimportant, but how you work out seating is very significant. As you and the antagonist enter your office, simply take your seat, perhaps without inviting him or her to sit down. Eventually, the antagonist will sit, but for a brief moment will be uncertain whether he or she belongs there or not.

The height of your respective chairs is also important. Because sitting higher than another can give a slight but definite subliminal advantage in the situation, make sure the antagonist's chair is not higher than yours.

If your desk faces into the room, have the antagonist sit across the desk from you. Talking across a desk can provide emotional distance and a feeling of protection. It also sets an authoritative tone for you and sends the message that you are in control.

What about Coffee?

Should you offer coffee or not? This is another item that might seem of minimal importance, but offering a beverage is one way to make a person feel more comfortable. You don't want to do that with an antagonist. Forgo this gesture of hospitality, unless this would be very atypical for you.

How to Conduct the Meeting Itself

The following suggestions cover the heart of the conversation itself—what happens from the time the antagonist is first seated through the end of the interaction.

Who Should Talk First?

The preliminaries are over. The antagonist is seated, and the interaction is about to begin. Who should start the conversation? When dealing with antagonists, do not do what you would normally do. Resist the temptation to "bridge the gap" to get the conversation going. Don't say, "You mentioned that you wanted to talk to me about some concerns you had." Don't say anything at all. Let the antagonist speak first. Don't worry. He or she will have plenty to say, but there is no need to make it easy. Look silently at him or her but don't look expectantly or give any nonverbal cues. Why build a bridge over which the antagonist can walk to give you trouble?

How Much Should You Talk?

Many people talk too much when meeting with antagonists—perhaps from anxiety or a false assumption that reason and logic will help the antagonist see things correctly. With antagonists, however, your best course of action is to keep relatively silent. The more antagonists are able to engage you in conversation, the better off they are. Saying little and maintaining a solid presence (steady eyes, good posture, minimal fidgeting) is far more beneficial than words.

How Should You Listen?

Be an attentive listener, but not an active listener. Active listening involves using verbal and nonverbal cues, such as nodding your head, to encourage conversation. With an antagonist, you want to do the opposite. Any reinforcement, positive or negative, leads the antagonist to continue talking. Joel Greenspoon's classic research on operant conditioning supports this principle. Greenspoon set up fictitious interviews, instructing the interviewers to say, "Mmm-hmmm," each time the interviewee used a plural noun. He found that the subjects unconsciously began to use more and more plural responses as a result of this subtle conditioning.[1] Your use of verbal and nonverbal encouragement can also reinforce an antagonist's offensive.

How "Noteworthy" Is the Meeting?

Take notes when meeting with an antagonist. First, your notes will serve as a permanent record of the meeting—for future reference. Second, taking notes also relieves you from having to maintain constant eye contact. (Some eye contact is important, however, because it communicates your strength to the antagonist.)

---

[1] Joel Greenspoon, "The Reinforcing Effect of Two Spoken Sounds on the Frequency of Two Responses," *American Journal of Psychology*, vol. 68 [1955]: 409-416.

Proper documentation of any interaction with an antagonist is vital for future disciplinary measures. Note the date, who attended, specific topics discussed, resolution (if any), and other relevant facts.

What about Recording the Meeting?

It probably would be unwise to record an interview with an antagonist. It would be incendiary as well as nonproductive. Telling the antagonist you intend to record the interview further escalates the importance of the encounter, which you want to avoid.

If the antagonist asks to record the meeting, firmly decline. If the antagonist presumes to tell you he or she intends to record your meeting, say that you do not conduct meetings of two people intended for the benefit of an unseen audience. If the antagonist persists, just end the meeting.

How Do You Handle Questions?

Antagonists frequently ask questions to try to lure you into saying something they can use against you. Many questions are obviously hostile, and you will know exactly why the antagonist is asking them. But apparently harmless questions can also cause problems. For example, if you are a new staff person, an antagonist may ask, "How do you like it here?" Avoid answering in detail. This will give the antagonist less opportunity to misconstrue what you say or repeat your answer out of context. A good response to this sort of question is: "Fine." If the antagonist persists in trying to drag an opinion from you, continue to say "Fine" or "Great," or some other innocuous response.

How to Handle a One-to-One Meeting with an Antagonist

Sometimes an antagonist might ask you about something he or she would like to see done (or undone). For example, if the customer service department you supervise is doing something different, an antagonist might say: "Do you intend to change back to the old way of doing things?" Answer this type of question by saying something like, "This is the way the department has decided to do it." If the antagonist directly asks if something might change, say, "This is the way we're doing it." He or she might persist, saying something like, "I know full well that you have the power to make changes yourself." Neither confirm nor deny the antagonist's statement. Continue by saying, "This is the way we are doing it."

Sometimes an antagonist will ask questions to which either a yes or a no could give the antagonist ammunition. For example: "Don't you think the squabbling between the marketing department and the production department is shameful?" One way to answer is to say, "I hear you." Or you might say a very neutral "Oh." The antagonist may not want to accept such an answer and might persist, but remember that you are under no obligation to answer unfair or irrelevant questions—it is your right to answer or not answer a question as you please. Realizing how antagonists can twist such information, discretion is certainly the better part of valor.

Should You Challenge Antagonists?

Be firm with antagonists, but avoid challenging or arguing with them. Challenging or arguing with antagonists produces no good, and there is very little possibility that you can change their minds. You also run the risk of further agitating them, fueling their aggressive activity after the interview.

Take care also not to bait antagonists. Resist any temptation to make fun of them, even if they make ludicrous statements that tempt you to laugh as you simultaneously feel your anger rise. Your natural desire might be to respond sarcastically, but that only angers them more. Refrain from putting them down. You may need to bite your tongue, but a sore tongue is better than added fuel for an antagonist's fire.

If an antagonist tries to argue with you by falsely accusing you of something, answer firmly but don't continue to deny the same thing over and over. Set the record straight once, maybe twice, and then calmly say, "You've already heard what I said." Trying to reason with an antagonist is, as the saying goes, like mud-wrestling with a pig. You both get dirty, but the pig enjoys it.

When Do You Conclude?

Stick to whatever initial time frame you have established for the meeting. Don't extend the time when the antagonist says, "I have just one more point to make." You are a person with other responsibilities that need your attention. Remember that antagonists are insatiable. No amount of extra time will ever satisfy this individual or lead to the resolution of his or her concerns.

Guarding against Physical Danger

Perhaps the methods outlined in this chapter seem counterintuitive to you. Won't this firmness—giving the individual nothing to go on—just make the person angrier? Won't this simply fuel the fires? If you give minimal responses to

How to Handle a One-to-One Meeting with an Antagonist

antagonists, doesn't that encourage them to ever-greater frenzy and efforts to foment destruction?

But in fact, the methods described in this chapter and in the entire book are designed to turn down the heat antagonists need to keep stoked up. When you relate to antagonists in the way that this chapter lays out, the net result is to lower their operating pressure, not to empower them. These methods do not completely subdue antagonists, but they definitely subdue them better than trying to placate them does. Because the antagonist gets nothing from you—no encouragement, no reinforcement, no expression of vulnerability or defensiveness—he or she is left with less to fight with or against.

There are times—in the minority, thankfully—when you need to make short-term adaptations to these principles and practices. One of those times is when you have an idea that there may be imminent physical danger in a particular situation. Some of the same principles still apply—adopting a stance of calmness and respect—but others need to be modified for a dangerous situation.

If you think a person is potentially dangerous, follow the procedures set out in your organization for such situations. There are also other actions you might take ahead of time to defuse the possibility of violence. Consider referring the antagonist to someone else in the organization whom the antagonist may perceive as being more neutral. This could reduce his or her aggressiveness.

If you have followed the principles of proper identification of antagonists spelled out in earlier parts of this book, and the principles of prevention in chapters 17–19, you will reduce the likelihood of antagonism as well as of physical danger. Prevention is always less costly than having to come up with a cure.

Effectively handling meetings with antagonists requires three elements:

- *Work.* You must be willing to work hard to conduct the interview according to these principles.
- *Change.* You will be called on to act in ways that might not appear to be caring or natural for you. Trust the process and courageously try out new behaviors.
- *Belief.* Believe that what you are doing is right and act in accordance with that belief.

CHAPTER **14**

Organizational Communications Regarding Antagonism

WHEN ANTAGONISTS ARE ACTIVE, leaders frequently are tempted to turn to the various organizational communication channels available to them to try to settle the conflict, to inform the department (or the whole organization) about the problems an antagonist is causing, or—most tempting and most futile—to communicate indirectly with the antagonist with the hope that he or she will get the message and change.

From a memo by the vice president of the marketing and sales division:

> "It has come to my attention that there are some in this division who disagree with certain policies set forth by management. If anyone is dissatisfied, he or she should speak with me first. There are appropriate channels for expressing disagreement. Spreading untruths and dissension are not among them."

From a speech offered by the president of a small company at the annual picnic:

Part Two: Dealing with Antagonists

> "This has been a good time for us today. It is an example of how we need to get along all the time instead of quarreling and infighting. I hope we can be open and up-front with each other, always putting the best construction on everything."

From an employee newsletter, an article titled "A Word to the Wise" by the CEO:

> "We're in the business of making newspapers. She reports, he typesets, some print them, others distribute them. All of us make newspapers and sell them. We don't have time to engage in bickering, rumor-mongering, or fighting. When we fall into these behaviors, we make and sell fewer papers, and that has job security implications for all of us."

One manager shared with me the futility of these kinds of communications: "Each time I tried to communicate indirectly to an antagonist through e-mail or memos to the whole department, it did nothing to effect a change in the antagonist. Instead, it caused unrest and resentment among those the indirect message was *not* intended for." Other leaders who tried to reach—and change—an antagonist through indirect channels also found these methods of communicating to be unproductive. One manager called this "supervising the herd" instead of dealing with an antagonist.

Communications of this sort hold a certain appeal. On the surface, they seem to confront the problem directly, but using organizational channels of communication to combat antagonism is usually unsuccessful for a number of reasons.

Organizational Communications Regarding Antagonism

- *It gives the antagonist attention and recognition, in some ways actually reinforcing the negative behavior.* Despite your intentions, the antagonist may relish the publicity. He or she may be overjoyed at your acknowledgment. You may feed a martyr complex, which thrives on what the antagonist perceives to be verbal or written persecution. On the other hand, the antagonist might feel threatened, pushed into a corner, and increasingly angry. By arousing his or her ire, you throw gasoline on the antagonist's fire. Either way you lose.

- *It could be perceived as taking unfair advantage of your position.* Even those who agree with your assessment of a given situation might frown on your use of internal organizational communication channels to try to deal with the matter. It might appear that you are taking unfair advantage of your position, despite the fact that the antagonist has probably been unfair to you as well as others.

- *"Getting tough" in a public memo or through other organizational channels can present you in a bad light.* Publicly venting your anger or frustration is as ineffective as venting your fears. It only serves to make people afraid of you—and you don't want to scare away your supporters. Granted, probably no one will think you are a weak leader, but demonstrating that kind of strength is undesirable.

- *It can create doubt where there was none before.* Shakespeare expressed it this way in *Hamlet:* "The lady doth protest too much, methinks." When people defend themselves publicly, the "public" may start to wonder why.

Part Two: Dealing with Antagonists

The individual who stands before a group and says, "I have been accused, though not to my face, of _____, but I want you all to know that it is not true," plants doubt where none may have existed previously. So does the manager who announces, "There are those who would like to see me gone." Nothing is to be gained by such public pronouncements.

- *It creates an unhealthy atmosphere for the whole department or organization.* Many employees might be blissfully unaware that anything is wrong. Once you go public, however, you make everyone aware of the unfortunate situation, or partially aware, which is worse. You create pain and anxiety for many who are helpless to do anything about the situation anyway, as well as increase conjecture and gossip.

- *By alluding to antagonism through organizational communication channels, you can appear to be weak.* If you reveal deep and intensely personal feelings on the matter, you can elicit disrespect from some individuals who aren't antagonists. Many people are unprepared to deal with that level of openness. There is also the question of appropriateness. There are proper times and places to share feelings, and there are times and places not to share them. Such sharing can be frightening, and those whom you lead might misunderstand. By doing this, you can diminish yourself in others' eyes—appearing unable to control yourself, much less able to function effectively as a leader.

- *It violates the use for which these communication channels were intended.* A speech by the CEO is a time for lifting up a vision for the company, not the place to vent emotions or hurl venomous arrows at an antagonist. Newsletters and e-mails are for communicating information, for networking, and for offering encouragement.

When the time is right, deal with antagonists directly. Save organizational communication channels for their intended uses.

CHAPTER 15

Personal and Family Variables

Antagonists not only affect you in the workplace but at home as well. You may become irritable or preoccupied and have difficulty listening or paying attention to your family's needs. You may be troubled by physical ailments, from headaches to sexual dysfunction. Your family's economics may suffer. At its worst, antagonistic conflict at work may even lead to marital or family difficulties.

Here is how some targets of antagonistic attacks described their experiences.

- "My thoughts consumed me, so I was distant from my family. The trouble caused me always to feel on edge. I had stomach upset and difficulty sleeping. I talked about it all the time with my wife, who didn't know how to advise me nor could she understand why I was so overwhelmed by this situation."

- "I carried all the anger home with me. I talked to my husband at great length about it. The result? More and more anger. My husband began to hate my job and everyone I worked with."

- "My family was worried about me and worried about our future. We felt so drained that we didn't have the energy and focus to cope with other problems. I constantly awoke in the middle of the night, ruminating about the situation, and could not get back to sleep. The sleep deprivation compounded my anxiety."
- "I spent so much time thinking about what was happening at work that I couldn't stay focused when my children tried to talk to me. I knew I was not being a good parent to them. Then I'd feel guilty because they deserved better than that."
- "Most of the laughter and play at home was replaced with general upset. Quarrels were more frequent. I was depressed and had no interest in doing anything with my family. I gained weight as food became my solace. My blood pressure rose. The situation threatened to become all-consuming."

Protecting Yourself

The effects of an antagonist's attack can threaten to overwhelm your self-confidence and self-esteem. You can find yourself wallowing in feelings of worthlessness and incompetence. You may have difficulty focusing on your regular work responsibilities. Your whole life, not just your work life, may seem out of control and confused.

It's rather common for those experiencing an antagonist's attack to come to the point where they doubt their own sanity from time to time. M. Scott Peck in *People of the Lie* speaks of how these people often create an aura of confusion in their intended victims, making them much more vulnerable. In the midst of the chaos an antagonist brings into your life, protecting yourself and protecting your family become both a practical necessity and a real challenge.

Find Stress Relievers

Even a relaxing vacation on a beautiful beach is of limited value if the same antagonistic turmoil and stress is awaiting your return. With that as a precaution, then, here are some suggestions for taking care of yourself until the situation is resolved:

- Schedule time for yourself. Relax by doing what you like to do—hobbies, reading, listening to music, and so on.
- "Move a muscle, change a thought." This bit of folk wisdom can be helpful. Some form of physical activity can help to ease your emotional overload—plus it is good for you! Schedule your exercise as you would any appointment—and keep it.
- If stress is affecting your health, seek appropriate medical help to deal with it.
- Put yourself in laughter's way. Whatever makes you laugh, arrange it. Rent a funny movie or go see the monkeys at the zoo.
- Be open to seeking the assistance of a counselor or your organization's Employee Assistance Program.

The real solution, of course, is to deal effectively with the antagonist—the sooner, the better.

Part Two: Dealing with Antagonists

Find a Coach or Confidant

You can receive invaluable assistance from a coach or confidant, someone with whom you can share feelings, thoughts, and strategies for coping with an antagonistic situation.

One reason—and no small one—that it's important to find a person to serve as coach or confidant is to protect your loved ones from being the sole repository of your anxiety, frustration, even anger. You need to be able to vent your feelings without exposing your family to this corrosive drain on their good will. And make no mistake—encounters with antagonists are like being splashed with acid.

Whether you find one or more persons to serve as coach or confidant within your organization or outside of your work situation, they should possess these three characteristics:

1. They need to fully understand the principles of confidentiality, and you must trust them to abide by these principles.
2. They need to exhibit a degree of personal sensitivity and understanding. The last thing you need is someone whose idea of good advice is to tell you, "Buck up. Keep a stiff upper lip." or "Ignore them, and they'll go away." They won't.
3. They need to be strong enough and knowledgeable enough about antagonists to support you in this crisis. Sharing this book with them, for instance, would give them needed information about antagonists.

When you find those whom you believe meet these criteria, you may still need to be somewhat circumspect, especially if they are from your organization. You may not want to share your deepest feelings about the antagonist—your desire to "squeeze his neck until his beady little eyes pop out," for example. Permit yourself some show of emotion, but don't go overboard.

Having a coach or confidant gives you the opportunity to express your frustration and anguish. He or she may be able to provide a different perspective on your situation and offer some good advice on dealing with the antagonist, perhaps even from personal experience.

Protecting Your Family

Although the catalog of ways family relationships can suffer is long, there is a more important question to address: What can you do to protect your family? Prevention is still the best antidote. If you head off antagonism before it becomes active in your work, you do more to shelter your family relationships than any after-the-fact "cures" will accomplish.

Even with the best of intentions, however, prevention is not always possible. If you are caught up in an antagonistic situation, here are some ways to protect your family from the stresses induced by antagonists.

- Warn your family that you are having a bad time at work, and that your preoccupation or shortness with them is the result of these pressures on you.
- Talk with your spouse and children—to a reasonable and proper extent—about what is happening. "Reasonable and proper" depends on your judgment and your children's ages. You need the support of your family, and your family needs the opportunity for growth through supporting you. At the same time, it is certainly possible to overwhelm

them. You need to rein in the tendency to rehash, rehearse, and reiterate what's going on at work. One person shared with me the rules he imposed on himself: "I would allow myself no more than 10 minutes' talk at home about the latest developments at work in my situation with the antagonist." Talking with a coach or confidant can provide you with an outlet for some of your more explosive emotions without involving your family.

- Encourage your spouse to find someone to talk with as well.
- Be aware of your feelings and keep communication open within your family.
- Share positive aspects of your work life as well as negative ones. If your family hears only negative reports from you, they might start seeing your work as the enemy.
- Schedule recreational time with your family and be firm about honoring the commitment. Look for activities that demand your total attention. One manager I know found that riding a roller coaster at a nearby theme park was an ideal way to take his mind off his stressful situation.

In the midst of your personal dealings with an antagonist and the accompanying turmoil, strive to minimize the damage an antagonist causes to you and your loved ones. You may not be able to carry out all these suggestions, but do what you can. Any such action will have positive results because you are exercising at least some control over how much an antagonist affects your personal life and relationships.

CHAPTER 16

The Aftermath

It's over. The long, arduous battle with the antagonist has finally ended. As you and other leaders survey the landscape, reminders of the struggle meet your eyes. You may wonder how you can heal the hurts and move beyond the recent troubles to a brighter future. This chapter focuses on what to do if some organizational repair work is needed.

Care for Others

In the aftermath of an antagonistic situation, many need care. Certainly others who had been on the front lines of attack have emotional wounds that require prompt treatment. They need you to listen to them, to give them encouragement and reassurance. They need to hear, "You did well; we never could have done it without you." Such listening and affirmation go a long way toward helping people sort out their jumbled feelings.

Aside from the frontline casualties, there are also civilian injuries. Offer care to the confused, innocent bystanders, employees who might be at a loss to understand what happened.

Employees who might have been followers of the antagonist also require attention. Most likely, they are feeling qualms of realistic guilt. Don't gloss over that guilt with a superficial, "Oh, that's all right!" It's not all right. They were part of the problem. Treat them with reserve at first, and make clear your expectations of them. Be fair but be cautious.

The list of casualties needing attention may be long. You're apt to identify most everyone who needs care, with one possible exception: yourself.

Care for Yourself

In numerous conversations and interviews with individuals who have suffered antagonistic attacks—leaders, managers, supervisors, and employees—I have discovered one constant: Rarely did these persons mention caring for themselves as part of the aftermath. After an antagonistic ordeal, you need to heal as well. In some ways what you have been through is analogous to the experiences that produce stress in war veterans and other victims of violence. Pages 134–135 in chapter 15 mention the value of acquiring a coach or confidant during an antagonistic attack. After the situation has been resolved, you might still find such counsel beneficial both personally and professionally.

Relating to the Antagonist

Through concerted efforts, you and other leaders have met the challenge of the antagonist's attack. What stance do you now take toward the antagonist if that person's employment was not terminated? How do you relate to that person in the aftermath? You might wish he or she would simplify your life by leaving the organization, but don't count on it. What do you do if he or she stays? Much of chapter 18, "Relating to Dormant Antagonists," can also apply to this situation.

As someone with a job to do, wiping the slate clean and starting over fresh will probably be uppermost in your mind after an antagonistic situation has ended. Were it only ordinary debate or disagreement now ended, even though accompanied by very strong feelings, I would unhesitatingly agree with that approach. But an antagonist, unfortunately, requires a different approach. Treat the person fairly, but don't be naive. Offer equality of treatment with open eyes—and a functioning memory.

It is vital to remember there is no such thing as a "former" or "past" antagonist. A more accurate term might be *antagonist in remission*—an antagonist who, though active in the past, is at the present time inactive. An antagonist can be compared to a volcano. A volcano is a volcano, whether it rumbles, spewing rock and ash, or appears silent and serene, puffing a little smoke now and then. Don't be duped by all that serenity. What is happening on the surface is not as important as what is inside. In dealing with a dormant antagonist, be every bit as careful as you would be in dealing with a volcano that erupted recently and is still smoking.

Let the Past Be the Past

Leaders who weather an antagonistic battle together are often tempted to refer to it constantly or joke about it incessantly. But after a while such continual conjuring up of the ghosts of antagonists can become downright wearisome and tend to strain relationships.

The idea of holding a departmental meeting with various staff levels present to go over the whole episode might seem appealing. Most of the time, however, this kind of review is equivalent to picking at a scab.

There is a place for review in leadership meetings, however, both as catharsis and to prepare against a recurrence. The recovery period is the ideal time to consider realistically how to avoid a repeat performance. For example, if the policies or procedures of the organization are unclear or have a significant gap through which the antagonist walked with ease, now is the time to update them, making them less subject to manipulation.

The aftermath of an antagonistic attack will find individuals especially anxious to prevent further disruptive and destructive situations. Now is a good time to take advantage of this teachable moment by strengthening general education about antagonism (see chapter 19, pages 159–162).

Your objective should never be merely to restore the organization to its former state. On the contrary, from the first moments when you and the other leaders begin picking up the pieces, your goal should be to create an even healthier organization, one better prepared to deal with antagonists. When I practiced as a clinical psychologist, I was not content just to get my clients back on an even keel, to help them return to where they were before they came to me. I wanted them to go beyond that. Another psychologist expressed this view by saying that he saw himself not as a "head shrinker" but a "head expander." Following this idea, any organization whose only goal is to recover and return to its former condition is already slipping behind. Let your recovery process be aimed at "organization expanding," making yourselves stronger than you were before.

Now that the antagonistic situation has been resolved, your main theme needs to be: The past is behind us, we will learn from our mistakes, now let's get on with our work.

Incorporate into your leadership style a very positive and upbeat attitude. In any communication you make about the conflict or any other topic, speak confidently and firmly, with the warm certainty that the problem is behind you and the future is good.

In sum: Move on.

Part Three

Preventing Antagonism

CHAPTER **17**

How to Create and Maintain an Anti-Antagonist Culture

WHILE SOME ORGANIZATIONS APPEAR NOT TO BE BOTHERED BY ANTAGONISTS, others seem to attract and activate them. What in an organization's culture keeps antagonists from flourishing?

There is a saying that goes like this: When you're up to your neck in alligators, it's difficult to think about draining the swamp. Draining the swamp—and keeping it drained—is the subject of this chapter. Here are some measures an organization can take to create an anti-antagonist culture.

Establish an Effective Hiring Process

Your organization can save itself a world of trouble by not hiring antagonists in the first place. There are many resources on the hiring process that you can refer to for specific recommendations. But I offer this primary caution to follow in your hiring process: *Take the time you need to get it right.* Hiring determinations are among the longest-lasting decisions any manager makes, so any investment of your time and effort is certainly worthwhile.

Part Three: Preventing Antagonism

A number of supervisors I've talked with had some helpful ideas. "Have an applicant interview with multiple people," suggested the office manager of a clinic. A factory owner added, "Use peer interviewing. Sometimes people at the same level as the applicant can see things upper management cannot." A human resources professional said her favorite question to ask during an interview is this: "What kind of boss do you work well with?" Sometimes the answers can be quite revealing. A small business owner suggested, "Train staff in teamwork. A well-trained team will likely be less tolerant of antagonistic behavior and more willing to be open about the problem."

Very importantly, keep in mind the seven questions, pages 9–10, from the introduction, the definition of an antagonist in chapter 1, the personality characteristics in chapter 2, and the eighteen red flags of antagonists in chapter 3 as you evaluate applicants. It is far easier not to bring potential antagonists into your organization, regardless of how talented or skilled they are, than it is to repair the damage that is sure to come with their attacks.

Follow Established Policies and Procedures

Another good way to prevent antagonism is to have clear-cut, up-to-date, and concise policies and procedures in place and then for everyone to follow them in a fair and consistent manner. Some managers and leaders of an organization might be unaware of certain policies and procedures because they have never had a need to apply them. Before any problem arises, search out and learn your organization's way of handling difficult matters such as antagonism, and then follow these policies and procedures as quickly and fully as possible if an antagonistic situation develops.

"It takes more than just having policies and procedures," the CEO of an industrial plant told me. "Supervisors also need to be trained to use them correctly." Because of current legal standards, many organizations have a very flexible policy of complaint and dispute resolution, for example. With their seeming aptitude for circumventing procedures, antagonists may thus be able to bypass the usual chain of command in their quest to register a complaint "with someone in authority." It is vital for organizational leaders to recognize when this is happening for invalid reasons.

Maintain Clear Job Descriptions

Clear and current job descriptions create an unfavorable environment for antagonists. Job descriptions give order and structure in the face of antagonists, who thrive on disorder and structural weakness. Antagonists look for weak points. Their standard operating procedure is to create confusion by raising a smoke screen of lies and half-truths. Clear job descriptions lower the risk of antagonists capitalizing on ambiguity or lack of definition.

Along with current, accurate job descriptions, it is also vital to conduct active job reviews with clear-cut guidelines on how the review or evaluation will take place. Thoroughly written appraisals or evaluations of both performance and behavior would go a long way toward revealing—and maybe curbing—an antagonist.

Follow Disciplinary Guidelines

Functional disciplinary measures are essential to maintaining an anti-antagonist culture. Antagonists flourish when discipline is absent or inconsistently applied. Clear and consistent application of policies is key. Find out what your organization's disciplinary guidelines are before you need them. Then follow them meticulously when dealing with an antagonist.

"Create and maintain thorough documentation of performance-affecting behavior and its impact on the organization," a business owner suggested. "This can be a tedious task but is invaluable when the inevitable confrontation takes place." Such documentation should of course apply to all, not just antagonists. Complete documentation will demonstrate your fairness in your dealings with an antagonist or any other employee.

Provide Functional Feedback Channels

To more effectively thwart the development of antagonists in an organization, maintaining open and honest communication is vital. Leaders should clearly identify the appropriate channels of feedback and reinforce that frequently. When supervisors maintain an open door, inviting employees to come to them with any questions or concerns they have without fear of reprisal, then someone who is fomenting turmoil through rumor and innuendo is going to be more easily detected and exposed.

Practice Anticipatory Socialization

Another important technique by which leaders can minimize antagonism is the use of "anticipatory socialization." This is psychological shorthand for, "Let people know what you are planning to do before you do it."

The purpose of anticipatory socialization is to prevent individuals from being caught off-guard by impending changes. People tend to resist change, especially in matters that affect them personally. Letting employees know as far in advance as is possible and giving as much information as you can about prospective changes diminishes fear or anxiety and also reduces the opportunity for antagonists to complain, "They never let us know what is happening around here."

You have the best chance of creating an anti-antagonist culture if you are genuine and respectful of others, firm when firmness is called for, and scrupulously fair with every person. Be yourself—unless, of course, you happen to be an antagonist, in which case be someone else!

CHAPTER **18**

Relating to Dormant Antagonists

A PERSON WHO CLEARLY DISPLAYS RED FLAGS OF ANTAGONISM and other diagnostic indicators but is not presently sowing discord in the organization could be considered a dormant antagonist. This could be an individual whose behavior has just come to your attention or even a person whom you and other leaders have dealt with successfully in a prior antagonistic situation. Treating a dormant antagonist the same way you would an active antagonist would be inappropriate.

So what do you do? How should you relate to such an individual? The answer is *very, very carefully.* You should be no less fair and no less courteous in your behavior, but you need to be more careful. Your exact strategy and response will vary depending on the level of antagonistic behavior, but in all cases you will need to be on your guard. Certain early actions on your part can reduce the probability of unhealthy conflict, discord, and hurt later on.

Of the guidelines that follow, some are more appropriate for managers and supervisors; others apply equally to all employees, whatever their responsibilities.

Keep an Emotional Distance

Keep your emotional distance with an antagonist. Be professional, consistent, and self-controlled. Remain somewhat aloof. Don't run from antagonists when they are dormant, but avoid inviting them to sit at your hearth. (The vestibule or foyer is close enough.) Avoid close personal contact, but don't obviously shun them. Keep verbal communication brief and factual—avoid idle chatter.

When you relate to potential or dormant antagonists somewhat formally, they might sense a difference without being able to put a finger on it. Occasionally they might ask you, either directly or in a roundabout way, "Is something wrong?" At this point your answer should be a simple no. Nothing *is* wrong—so far. In the unlikely event that you misjudged them, you can always relate less cautiously as time goes on.

You might be concerned that restrained behavior will upset or disturb antagonists. It probably won't, but the issue is weighing short-term versus long-term results. Careful, reserved behavior now will reduce the chance that they will gain the upper hand and take advantage of you later.

Be Accurate

Make sure the information you share with an antagonist (or with an antagonist present) is accurate. Relating to antagonists in particular requires more accuracy than, "If I remember correctly," or, "I'm almost positive," or "Unless my memory fails me." Don't guess, estimate, or venture any off-the-cuff opinions to those you have determined may well be dormant antagonists. An educated guess about sales figures two years earlier, for example, might be acceptable to most people. To a potential antagonist seeking the same information, unless you are 100% certain, say something like, "I'll look it up and let you know." Antagonists are delighted by opportunities to prove others wrong—even slightly—and will seize any chance to catch you in an error.

Be similarly cautious about commenting on company policy matters. If an antagonist asks you about the interpretation of a particular policy or rule, offer to look it up, unless you are certain of the correct interpretation. Instant answers are not required for everything, especially an antagonist's unending irritating or tricky questions.

If you know a potential antagonist will be present at a given meeting, do your homework and be sure of your facts ahead of time. There is an excellent chance the antagonist will try to use what you say against you, so choose your words carefully and prepare thoroughly. With antagonists about, it's a matter of pay now—with thorough preparation—or pay more later, by being made to jump through the antagonist's hoops.

Avoid Excessive Positive Reinforcement

Of course you should avoid reinforcing the inappropriate behaviors of an antagonist. (Remember that it is a red-flag individual you are considering.) But even when such a person does something commendable, don't praise excessively.

Excessive praise involves at least three dangers: First, it raises an antagonist's view of him- or herself. Increasing the confidence of an antagonist feeds the emotional power base from which he or she can launch an attack on you or another leader.

Second, by excessively praising an antagonist in front of others, you make it easier for the antagonist to build a strong following. Like using a bank balance, he or she will draw on such special status to cause dissension and destruction later on. A simple thank-you, adequate to the occasion but too small to hoard, can minimize this danger. Third, excessive praise can make disciplining an antagonist troublesome. In the case of any legal action brought by an antagonist following his or her dismissal, for instance, defending against accusations of discrimination would be very difficult. The existence of excellent performance evaluations and constant praise can help antagonists convince juries that subsequent discipline is really just a "pretext" for discrimination.

The temptation to lavish praise on an antagonist is great because common reasoning states that if you take great pains to affirm a person, then he or she will respond by being very affirming of you. It doesn't work that way with antagonists. Give the antagonist as much praise as he or she deserves—but not one crumb more.

Hold On to Your Gauntlet

In the Middle Ages, knights issued challenges to one another by throwing down their gauntlets, the protective glove that was part of their armor. This was their way of saying, "Okay, let's have at it!"

In relating to a potential antagonist, do not throw down your gauntlet too soon. Have patience. An antagonist's actions must be significant enough to warrant confrontation; otherwise, you will appear belligerent. Until other leaders are fully on board with the understanding that the antagonist must be dealt with, wait. Timing is essential: Be sure the time is right because, when you do confront the antagonist fully, it is better to do so with the involvement of others.

Hold Your Tongue

In line with the preceding caution about timing, learn to hold your tongue even when an antagonist is provoking you. The point is, don't react—*yet*. The time to deal with the antagonist will come. Responding too soon gives the antagonist the satisfaction of knowing he or she has upset you.

When you respond to the taunts and charges of troublemakers, they've got you from the start. From an attacker's point of view, the attack is worthwhile only if it causes discomfort for another, and the only way the attacker can know he or she is successful is to see the victim respond indignantly or lose control. If you react defensively, you'll actually lose. As one person told me, "This is where I've seen leaders get into trouble. If a leader loses his or her temper, everyone focuses on that person's anger, rather than on the antagonist's underhanded tactics."

Following are some suggestions on how to deal with verbal abuse from an antagonist.

- The truth won't hurt you unless you let it. Sometimes an antagonist makes a statement that is absolutely true. In the course of a meeting, for example, an antagonist might address the chairperson and say, "After all, you didn't even join this organization until two years ago." An excellent response is an unembellished and assertive "That's right," or total silence, which can be quite powerful. Then move on to the next order of business. To respond by justifying yourself is not wise. Don't waste your time and energy; a response elevates the accusation to a significance beyond what it deserves. (See also "How to Handle Antagonists in Group Situations," pages 95–96.)

- Don't set up a special committee to handle the antagonist's accusations. Some people think that if they get three or four people together to listen to the antagonist's concerns, they can reach a peaceful resolution. This action only increases the apparent credibility and legitimacy of the antagonist's accusations and magnifies the very problem you want to nip in the bud. Committees tend to drag on and on, wasting everyone's time except the antagonist's, who relishes the attention. Chapter 12 of this book notes that there are times when powerful action by a group—one ready to deal with an antagonist—is in order, but not until you are sufficiently prepared to do so effectively.

Defend yourself against a potential antagonist's behavior by brushing it off as a petty annoyance—or better, no annoyance at all. Your attitude must communicate a sense of imperviousness to attack, as should that of the other leaders or groups within the organization. Antagonists are experts at the art of psychological warfare. If they can get you to feel and act fearfully or defensively in public, you are offering them the reward they want.

You have a choice: You can operate from strength early on, dealing with potential or dormant antagonists calmly and nondefensively, or you can react later when an antagonistic situation threatens to mushroom out of control. An ounce of prevention now is worth much more than a pound of damage control later.

CHAPTER **19**

Educating Others

Thomas Henry Huxley once said, "Perhaps the most valuable result of all education is the ability to make yourself do the thing you have to do when it ought to be done, whether you like it or not" ("Technical Education," 1877). Education indeed equips people to do what must be done, no matter how uncomfortable the task—and few tasks are more uncomfortable than doing what must be done to deal with antagonists. Education about antagonism falls into two categories: *general* information about antagonism and *specific* information that is focused on a particular person.

General Education

The goal of general education is to communicate an understanding of the dynamics of antagonism and ways to handle it effectively. Include as many leaders as possible in the general educational process—from the executive level to departmental supervisors and team leaders, as well as their support staff who may also have contact with antagonists.

Part Three: Preventing Antagonism

When should general education begin? Yesterday! It is never too soon. There are distinct advantages to initiating this process when it is not connected with a specific antagonistic crisis. You can treat the subject more dispassionately because you will be able to focus on the topic in a general way. You also reduce the possibility that others will think you are acting defensively or aggressively. As John Wooden has said, "The time to prepare isn't after you've been given the opportunity. It's long before that opportunity arises."[1]

Who initiates the task of general education? You do, or another appropriate person who cares about your organization or division and its effectiveness. You have already begun this process for yourself by reading this book. A next step could be to form an educational team or leadership group to read and discuss this book. Even if there are no antagonists currently nipping at your organization, most people will find education about antagonism to be valuable in many areas of their lives since antagonists also operate outside of the workplace.

There are two purposes of general education. The first is prevention. Leaders who are able to detect and identify antagonists are better equipped to lead and to take proactive steps to protect their department, division, or the organization as a whole from an antagonist's ravages. The second purpose is to provide a foundation for specific education when or if that step becomes necessary.

---

1 Wooden, John and Steve Jamison, *Wooden: A Lifetime of Observations and Reflections On and Off the Court* (Chicago: Contemporary Books, 1997), p. 130.

Specific Education

Specific education involves educating those who need to know about a particular individual who is beginning to behave antagonistically. Specific education should begin when a problem has been identified and one or more leaders have been attacked. Prior general education can help make specific education easier, but you or other leaders may need to nudge people's perceptions and alert them that the organization may be dealing with an antagonist.

Before tackling the subject, recognize how sensitive specific education is. You mention names. You discuss behaviors. Handle it with *extreme care.*

The purpose of specific education is twofold: First, leaders are enabled to assess the particular situation more accurately. Second, specific education paves the way for planning strategies to solve the problem.

Specific education differs from general education with respect to audience. *General education* should be available to as many people as possible, so they can be aware of the dynamics and treatment of antagonism. *Specific education* is for those who bear legitimate responsibility for handling and resolving the problem or those who are connected in some way. If your organization has specific policies and guidelines to handle disciplinary issues, educate the persons in the chain of command who are responsible for implementing these policies. Key support staff, who may also be contacted by an antagonist, should also be educated about the situation and possible solutions.

Handle specific education tactfully. It might be difficult to say: "Mr. (or Ms.) X is an antagonist," although sometimes the problem is so obvious that these words can be spoken and explained with ease. At other times, specific education should proceed slowly and inductively from effects to causes. Begin to inform selected leaders about ways antagonists usually act. Allow time for members of the group to study the definition of antagonism in chapter 1 and ask the seven diagnostic questions on pages 9–10 in the introduction. Refer also to the personality characteristics described in chapter 2 and the red-flag behaviors described in chapter 3. If necessary, point out patterns or tendencies evident in the antagonist. The more you let the facts about antagonism—and specific antagonists—speak for themselves, the more likely you are to be taken seriously.

Educating people in your organization about antagonists—their potential for harm and successful ways to deal with them—is especially important in creating and maintaining an anti-antagonist culture. Preventing antagonism in the first place or nipping it in the bud is much easier than dealing with the results of a full-blown attack.

CHAPTER **20**

The Last Temptation

WHEN YOU TURN THE FINAL PAGE and finish this book, you may face the temptation to shelve what you have learned along with the book itself. It is always difficult to cross the bridge from knowledge to action. Beneath that figurative bridge lives a whole family of trolls who will try to waylay you with reasons why you should not cross to the other side. The only way to silence these creatures is to confront every rationalization they offer with the truth. The truth, like the sun, will turn such trolls into harmless stones. Here are the lies those trolls will whisper and the truths you can bring to bear against them.

Troll 1: "You don't really think it will work, do you?"

As you read through this book, you probably heard from this troll more than once. A variation of this seductive blandishment is: "Maybe it would work for someone else, but not for you—it's not your style." This troll will insist, for example, that meeting with an antagonist whenever and wherever the antagonist wants will do more to help the situation than meeting with

Part Three: Preventing Antagonism

an antagonist at the time and place you determine. This troll might also whisper that keeping an antagonist as busy and involved as possible, with more and more responsibility, is the best thing to do—that the antagonist will be so busy he or she will not have time to be antagonistic. These are seductive lies.

Troll 2: "You don't want to feel uncomfortable, do you?"

Dealing effectively with antagonists entails involvement in situations where conflict necessarily takes place. The troll is right: Nobody wants to experience uncomfortable conflict. Despite the fact that many times conflict is necessary and results in better working conditions and greater justice, this troll is enough to scare off many. The best way to deal with it is to say: "I have made up my mind to do what is right, not what is comfortable, and you will never dissuade me."

Troll 3: "People are never as bad as all that, are they?"

After you complete this book, this troll will still be around, insisting that you are too judgmental. The key to silencing this troll is to lay the facts out on the table: "Okay, Troll 3, we'll let the facts decide if Person X is an antagonist. Let's go back to chapters 1–3 and see." Before you finish speaking, the troll will be silenced for good, and you can move on past it.

Troll 4: "People won't like you if you do these things."

Ouch! This troll knows how to hit where it hurts. No one wants to be disliked. You can silence this beast by pointing out that, in the short term, a few people may not be happy about the way you have to deal with an antagonist because they don't understand the situation. In the long term, however, you will gain their respect for your courageous leadership.

Troll 5: "Leaders don't attack."

This troll is wrapping two lies in three words. First, it is misrepresenting what you are advised to do in this book. Your goal is not to attack the antagonist, but to defend and protect the organization and those who work for it. By rendering the antagonist harmless or ejecting him or her from the organization, you accomplish this. The troll's second lie is a false conception of what a leader does. A leader's primary concern is for the welfare of the organization and its employees. Anyone or anything that threatens to disrupt the mission and purpose of the organization must be dealt with as quickly, fairly, and decisively as possible to protect the organization and maintain its health.

Troll 6: "No one will support you in this."

This may well be the biggest challenge you will face. You know what can be done when leaders work together: Antagonists can't acquire any momentum. You also know how effectiveness and productivity are impeded when other leaders are uncooperative. You may feel alone, without support—just the ammunition this troll needs to dissuade you from taking any definitive action. But inaction will undoubtedly cause greater pain than doing the right thing. So tell this troll that, even if others don't support you, you will exercise your responsibilities and continue to work for their cooperation.

Part Three: Preventing Antagonism

Troll 7: "But it's so much work!"

That's right. Dealing with antagonists involves much effort. It is hard work to change old habits and form new behaviors, especially when you are involved in a crisis situation. As a leader you will need to exert much self-discipline. But you can tell this troll (and yourself) that if you don't work hard now, there may be nothing left to work for later.

Dealing decisively with antagonists is the right thing to do. I encourage you to be a courageous leader. Cross the bridge from knowledge to action. Protect the mission of the organization. Protect the people who work with you. Last but not least, protect yourself.

Index

A

accuracy in communication, 152–53
accusations, antagonistic, 49
action plan, 87–90, 101–07
activists, 20
aftermath, 137–41
aggression, 23–24
Americans with Disabilities Act, 30, 106
antagonist in remission, 139
antagonistic behavior in group settings, 35–36, 91–96
    dealing with, 95–96, 155–56
Antagonists in the Church, 10
anti-antagonist culture, 145–49
anticipatory socialization, 148–49
antisocial personality, 29–30
appeasement, 105
argumentum ad ignorantium, 16
authoritarianism, 25–26
authority, 65, 106–07, 147

B

broken glass trail, 32
Burke, Edmund, 71
burnout, 15

C

coach or confidant, 134–35, 136, 138
communications, antagonistic, 52–53

Index

objective, 98–100
organizational, 125–29
conflict in organizations, 57–62
    antagonistic, 61–62
    healthy, 15–16, 57, 61
    levels of, 58–62
criticism, 15
Cuban missile crisis, 105

D

definition of antagonists, 16–18
delusions, 27–28
    kernel of truth, 28
    of grandeur, 27
    of persecution, 27
disciplinary measures, 87–90, 105–06, 112, 148
displacement, 64
distortion, 51
divide-and-conquer tactics, 97
documentation, 148
dormant antagonists, 139, 151–57

E

education, 159–62
    general, 78, 88, 102, 104, 159–60
    specific, 80, 104, 161–62
emotional distance, 152
Employee Assistance Program (EAP), 106, 133
enlisting support from staff, 104
extension, 16
extinction, 102–03

F

family, effects on, 131–32, 134, 135–36
feedback channels, 148

G

Greenspoon, Joel, 119

H

Hamlet, 127
hard-core antagonists, 18
Henry V, 16
hiring process, 145–46
honeyed "concerns," 45
"Honorable Opposition," 16
Human Rights Acts, 30
Huxley, Thomas Henry, 159

I

indispensable antagonists, 81–90
invisible antagonists, 77–80
irritating questions, 45

J

Jamison, Steve, 102, 160
job descriptions, 147

K

Kennedy, John F., 105
kernel of truth, 28

L

leadership strategies, four specific, 101–07
Leas, Speed, 58–61
legal issues, 30, 41–42, 87–89, 106, 154
listening to antagonists, 119
lobbying, 53–54

M

major antagonists, 19
mavericks, 83–84
meddling, 47

meetings with antagonists, 109–24
Melanchthon, Philipp, 40
Menninger, Karl, 31
mobilizing the management team, 97–100
moderate antagonists, 19–20

N

narcissism, 22–23
negative self-concept, 21–22
Niemoeller, Martin, 71–72

O

objectivity, 98–100
operant conditioning, 119
organizational structure, 66–67, 145–49

P

paranoia, healthy, 31
paranoid personality, 26–28
passive aggression, 24
Peck, M. Scott, 62, 132–33
People of the Lie, 62, 132–33
personal and family variables, 131–36
protecting your family, 135–36

Index

protecting yourself, 132–35
personality characteristics, 21–30
  aggression, 23–24
  authoritarianism, 25–26
  narcissism, 22–23
  negative self-concept, 21–22
  psychiatric syndromes, 26–30
    antisocial personality, 29–30
    paranoid personality, 18, 26–28
    psychopathy, 29
    psychosis, 18
    sociopathy, 29–30
  rigidity, 24–25
pestering, 51–52
pettifogging, 16
phalanx, 88, 101–04
physical danger, 122–24
policies and procedures, 146–47
positive reinforcement, excessive, 153–54
pot-stirring, 45–46
pretense, 53
projection, 28
psychiatric syndromes, 26–30
  antisocial personality, 29–30
  paranoid personality, 18, 26–28
  psychopathy, 29
  psychosis, 18
  sociopathy, 29–30
psychotherapy and counseling, 27, 105–06

R

reasons for antagonism, 63–67
red flags of antagonism, 31–42
  aggressive means flag, 38
  cause flag, 40–41
  different drummer flag, 39
  extraordinary likability flag, 36
  flesh-tearing flag, 38–39
  gushing praise flag, 35
  "I gotcha" flag, 35–36
  instant buddy flag, 34–35
  job hopper flag, 36–37
  liar flag, 37
  nameless others flag, 33–34
  note-taker flag, 38
  parallel track record flag, 33

pest flag, 39–40
predecessor put-down flag, 34
previous track record flag, 32
school of hard knocks flag, 41
situational loser flag, 40
research, 7–8, 10
resistance, antagonistic, 47–48
rights and responsibilities, 70–71
rigidity, 24–25
Robert's Rules of Order, 93

S

sarcasm, 38–39, 44
self-concept, 21–22
seven diagnostic questions, 9–10
Shakespeare, 16, 127
"silent knife," 77
sixth sense, 55
sloganeering, 48–49
smirking, 51, 94
sociopathy, 29–30
sources of information, 54–55
special committee, 156
spying, 49–50
support for antagonists, 65–66

T

tactics and maneuvers of antagonists, 43–55
temptation, 163–66
Thirteen Days, 105
transference, 64–65
trolls, 163–66
types of antagonists, 18–20
    hard-core, 18
    major, 19
    moderate, 19–20

V

values, 69–73
verbal abuse, dealing with, 155–56

W

why antagonism happens, 63–67
Wooden, John, 102, 160

Z

Zulu saying, 97

About the Author

KENNETH C. HAUGK received a Ph.D. in clinical psychology from Washington University and an M.Div. from Concordia Seminary in St. Louis, Missouri. He is a member of the American Psychological Association, the Society of Consulting Psychology, and the Society of Psychologists in Management. He has practiced as a clinical psychologist and has taught psychology and leadership courses at several universities, as well as continuing education seminars through Washington University.

He is founder and Executive Director of Stephen Ministries, an organization that trains leaders to train others to provide one-to-one caregiving for those in various life crises or to lead small groups. Since 1975, the organization has trained over 50,000 leaders in its one-week leadership courses.

Dr. Haugk has written numerous books and professional articles on leadership, antagonism, assertiveness, critical thinking, experimental design, psychological testing, and community mental health. A frequent keynote speaker and workshop presenter on dealing with antagonists and other leadership topics, he has spoken extensively to business groups, health professionals, church groups, and not-for-profit executives.

If you are interested in Dr. Haugk's speaking at an event or conducting a workshop for your organization, you can contact him at:

Kenneth C. Haugk, Ph.D.
2045 Innerbelt Business Center Dr.
St. Louis, MO 63114-5765
(314) 428-2600
www.leaderkillers.com